Brooklyn Birth:
Sicilian Soul

One Man's Journey

Millennium Edition 2014

F. Anthony D'Alessandro

Goose River Press
Waldoboro, Maine

Copyright © 2014 F. Anthony D'Alessandro

All rights reserved. No part of this book may be reproduced in any form without written permission from the publisher, except by a reviewer who may quote brief passages in a review to be printed in a newspaper or magazine.

Library of Congress Card Number: 2014902336

ISBN: 978-1-59713-138-4

First Printing, 2014

Published by
Goose River Press
3400 Friendship Road
Waldoboro ME 04572
e-mail: gooseriverpress@roadrunner.com
www.gooseriverpress.com

DEDICATION

Dedicated to the special women in my life,
without whom, I'd never developed literacy,
without whom, I'd never developed *simpatico*,
and, without whom, I'd never have found inspiration,
nor discovered my elusive and reclusive voice.

Thanks to *la mamma*, born beneath the Cyclops' cliffs,
who never, ever tired of telling
and retelling folk tales to her wide-eyed, late life "child of
exhausted loins," her youngest son.
Equally significant in the poet's development was my muse,
a gift from God to lead me out of life's gutters: Adele.
Flaunting the genetics of a dazzling and brilliant daughter of
Dublin's past, a child of Lone Star's San Antonio,
she inspired the lyric to my writing and added a near lifelong aria
to my days, along with a magical melody that whispered from her
soul. Adele helped shape and guide verses that would have found
their home scratched and carved into cement city
pavements. Literary publications on these pages are basically due to
these two women, and a few others: my siblings, and especially Dr.
Mary Jo, along with cameo assists provided by dozens of gifted and
unsainted, unsmiling nuns who literally hammered formal
education into the poet's scattered imagination.
Gratitude goes to the Holy Spirit too for whispering ideas that
inspired these poems.

Chapter Headings:

1. Spirituall/Religious
2. Childhood
3. Places
4. Daddy Daze
5. Nostalgia
6. Grandchildren
7. Seniors
8. School
9. Attitudes/Encounters
10. Emerald Isle

Spiritual/Religious

Who Will Say the Rosaries Now?

She slumped and stared at the frazzled, shedding rocker embracing her.
Raising her spirit skyward, she waited.
Grandma waited.
She waited as her world orbited her.
The bride, blood of her blood, rerouted her wedding day photo op,
and instead, presented wedding bouquets, exchanged for Nona's blessing
and the familiar, "I love you Dolly."
Children and grandchildren from diverse locales such as the Eternal City, Country Music Capital, City by the Bay, and the Nation's Capital all checked in daily with this matriarch.
This astute daughter of Pirandello nurtured some resourceful scions.
Each of them reported Grandma's news directly to her
and quietly awaited her approval,
along with the shower of little kisses she rapid fired on their hands,
cheeks, or any accessible facial part.
Her actions were accented by, "*A cent'anni.*"
Sentenced to physical imprisonment
between an unraveling wicker rocker
and a tired bed during her sunset years, she survived and thrived anyway.
The spirit branded on her soul by her native Sirocco sun transcended the shackles of bedpost and rocker domains.
Brandishing her rosary bracelet, stretched to save souls
while sitting in that webbed chair,
pleading directly on her beaded prayer line to Paradise.
Twenty-seven rosaries recited each day.
Some don't ever recall seeing Nona without her fingers traversing,

marching bead to bead while mumbling *sotto voce*
until she reached the end of her rhythmic, spiritual Braille.
The twenty-seven rosaries represented a total of twenty-seven children,
grandchildren, and great-grandchildren.
She was the ultimate egalitarian.
An equal opportunity prayer distributer.
The generous, the good, the gifted, the gaudy, the greedy, and the gauche...
those who benefitted from life's genetic roulette
as well as those shortchanged
of integrity and intelligence at God's creation assembly line,
all shared an equal allocation of prayers.
So often her plaintive nonagenarian eyes concealed nimble fingers, and a racing mind
while navigating her sacred course along the highway of her holy beads.
The poet said at her eulogy, "She generously offered us all the gift of faith."
Sadly, her prodigal decedents perched on the ledges of shallow lives,
who managed to trample her gift, are doomed to
model lives of laughter-free emptiness, while the inheritors,
those of her bloodline who truly cared and captured her legacy will
soar with their sponsoring angel.
I still wonder though, who will say the rosaries for us now?
I can only suspect.

Arba Sicula (Sicilian Dawn) 2001

By His Stripes

I begged.
I pleaded.
I promised.
I prayed...
My private leprosy,
my personal curse,
reckless, fiery craters ravaged my skin.
Doggedly, persistently, stubbornly launched sneak attacks,
defiantly deflecting my prayerful attempts to douse.
Uninvited, new, crimson sand dunes dotted
and rudely squatted on my skin.
Doctors failed, while hope and faith retreated.
A hallow, desperate cry invoked one last prayer.
Providentially, a century old book
touting a timeless message drifted across my life.
Written by an inspired, obscure cleric, it sprawled
perched atop a freshly painted shelf, in a modern bookstore.
The book summoned me to attention.
Reluctantly, I bought the classic tome.
Its message: clear, simple, and truthful.
"BY HIS STRIPES I AM HEALED."
I was.

Broken Streets...1994

Persistent Provider

Have you ever noticed that when you collect beach shells
with children, no matter how many visitors have dredged
the same sands with their hungry fingers before you,
no matter how late you arrive at the scene,
there are always shells on lay away for you?
When you sense all hope flickering
a fresh wave, a surge of tide redeposits
another store of shells, and you're provided for.
I have a hunch that throughout life, without realizing it,
we are similarly provided with life's abundance,
even when we're last on line.

St. Joseph's Messinger, Spring 2003

Childhood

Foul Ball

It rushes and cleaves the skyscraper sky,
rotates, rolls, spins over and over,
white, bright, and neatly stitched.
The signature spin, it's meant for you only.
The other 50,000 fans are eliminated from this
preordained lottery.
The five score souls in your section don't matter either.
Your name is stitched in destiny as the baseball
threads and slices its way thru the ponderous August night sky.
You stare along the stadium's top ring.
You realize immediately, this one has a chance.
This one is yours.

The sphere spirals downward.
Arms, hands, flap, wave rudely,
reach out to invade your space.
Such futility: to tamper with the Fates.
You know when it's meant for you.
The ball coils, grows bigger,
finds your hand and screws itself into your palm.
It stings into your smile.

Jones Av. Poetry Review, June, 1998/Baseball Bard, 2013

Baseball Mitt

I remember my first new baseball glove.
I'd been through all of the hand-me-downs
from cousins, uncles, friends, even from
silver spooned uptown acquaintances.
Somehow that parade of gloves proved similar
to the half dozen fatigued and rusted
automobiles handed me a decade later.
They appeared effective and efficient for a few calendar
pages, then totally broke down.
And so it was with the gifts of tired, tattered, torn,
and discarded baseball mitts.
Then my big brother Peter drove me to a local
sporting goods store, Davega. Whatever became of them?
Probably occupying the same department store limbo
as E.J. Korvette and S. Klein stores.
He said, card dealing style, "Pick a mitt!!! Any mitt!!!"
I snatched the box wrapped around my choice off the shelf.
The Stan Musial, PMN model glove matched up to any I'd seen.
Just as my high back sneakers sporting the Circle K
possessed the magical elixir of flight, my PMM Glove
would transform me into a budding Stan Musial.
Kids in my Brooklyn days didn't just buy mitts and play.
There was a quasi-religious ritual attached
to "breaking-in" the mitt.
One preened it, one punched it, Marciano style.
One drenched it in Neatsfoot Oil.
One squeezed a ball into its pocket,
tied it tighter than a tourniquet
strangling it with rope.
Finally, one placed it under a mattress and slept on it.
All this preparation designed to develop the deep pocket,
so one would never drop a baseball.

You see, the glove was an admission ticket
to the diamond dream.
And, even when that dream dissolved to stardust,
it was all still worth the ritual.

Stoopball Slicksters

I stood on the same stoop that beckoned me as early as my diaper days.
Simpler days when life delivered new laughs, new friends, and surprises every day.
I'd stood on that once monstrous stoop while Dad first pointed out Santa
and his reindeer streaking across an ice cold Canarsie Christmas sky.
A wide-eyed six year old, I'd bought into that fantasy tale.
My dad convinced me that I'd seen old St. Nick on his gift run, above Brooklyn's Bridge.
That stoop served as my podium, as I'd chatted with this familiar moon,
during my pocked faced days.
The same stars who'd served as celestial lighthouse to that childhood Santa,
blinked at me tonight, while some of the same muscular trees sheltered me again.
Those oaks now as wrinkled as aging elephants,
with a graffiti collection of dried up love initials,
rustled their leaves to salute my return.
The same stoop now stretched into the 21st century continued to ignore me.
The stoop's brick and concrete competed with my cratered face in the creviced
and lined category.
The seasoned stoop flaunted age spots, cracks, and suffered from masonry leprosy.
The tired and peeling front door with two score years of annual layers of paint
groping it, stood without the mouth watering aroma of tantalizing spaghetti sauce

sneaking past its ample supply of fissures.
I suppose much like aging humans, in our near half century separation,
the stoop, no longer monstrous, seemed to have shrunk to half the size
it once occupied in my memory.
Most familiar Brooklyn stoop ball legends from the past century,
and their fans faded into eternity, all victims of the book of days,
along with their baggage of dreams.
Compelled by a stalking curiosity to revisit my childhood home,
this homecoming spiked with thick layers of melancholy.
I sprawled on tired old stoop, hoping to feel some welcome,
and invitation to sit and relax.
The classic black DeSoto motorcar ,once reminiscent of exotic cats
protecting Pharaoh's tombs, no longer lounged in front of its stoop.
Now pretenders, anorexic, runty cars, not appearing full grown,
two in fact, squatted on DeSoto's reserved parking platform.
Dreams of my athletic glory spawned on this old brick stoop.
With the help of my trusted rubber ball, the familiar, slouching street light,
and stoop served as the only prop needed to play all-night ball.
During those sweaty Brooklyn trolley days, life was as simple as a broom stick,
taped and covered with black electric tape, a Spaldeen rubber ball,
and a stoop to bounce a ball off.
Despite the complaint of that growling, toothless, ball-snatching survivor
from Flanders Fields living on the other side of the street,
we played on and on thru the night.
I now realized that I'd probably witnessed far more sunrises than that grumpy,
thieving rubber ball collector. Ironic?
After marathon games, the stoop served as a stage where we clowned with friends

and family under star and moon backdrop.
Tonight it's reduced to four...the stars, moon, and stoop that surround me.
The curtain closed on all stoop ball play here last century,
as well as any lingering dreams of stadium celebrity.
Now only the ghosts of local, legendary past players pop to mind.
But, I remember this old moon, the storied stars, and yes,
relocated stars, and the magnificence in their sparkle.
Not so with stoop or this slower motion interloper now sprawled on stoop.
The lightning quick boy who once occupied this frame, who had pounded stoop
with his flurry of rubber balls is merely a distant recollection.
As I stare, I reminisce about stoop and her lovingly abusive pals:
Allegro Alberto sleeps eternally in some Asian bog.
Crazy Cal, the catcher, briefly heard the roars of full house stadium crowds
until his right eye met a stray baseball that shattered his vision and diamond dream.
Lefty legend Capp's shotgun arm misfired, and now others strain to plant flowers
above his resting place at slumbering speeds.
Loony Louie discovered the divine and stumbled onto an epiphany.
Now, he's Gentle Lou of the cloth and collar.
Sexy Sue, a top ranked stoop ball star,
shed all traces of her descriptive adjective in the Seventies.
Big Bro, who designed the loop my curve ball, soft tosses with Gabriel's angelic team.
No more pleas like, "Wanna play catch kid?"
No more, "Walk me to the candy store."
No more, "C'mon let's get an egg cream."
My task today is to scrub the flaking, tired house,
preparing for her remaining new Millennium days.
Who thought that someday I'd be sacrilegiously sitting in my

Pop's sacred spot,
sans vino, flaunting more silver mane than he ever had.
Well, it's time to toss out the well worn scraps of the past,
package physical remains of memories and sweep away a junk
pile brimming with the fragments of my life.
The moment has come to gut the very soul of this house,
along with its breathtaking "This is Your Life" flavor.

Riversedge, University of Texas, 2011

Mud Puddle Reminiscences

I raised my brow, stared into my rear view mirror and smiled.
My car's wake sliced the mud puddle that I'd aroused
on the apron of the construction site.
Weird, but throughout my cavalcade of years,
I'd never lost my fascination for mud puddles.
A clown-like smile commandeers my face as I think back to the six-year-old me
plopped in the center of an urban, curbside pool, intently sailing my wooden
ice cream sticks to safe harbor across these pothole canals and oceans.
When the green giant Brooklyn bus inched up to its rest stop, the spindly legs of my youth
grasshoppered me to the safety of the cracked, craggy city sidewalk.
All that while, I still managed to smugly monitor the new turbulence developing
in my private ocean resulting from the bus tire's rhythmic massage.
Those bulging bus tires on steroids, towered a foot above my toddler head
during those Brooklyn days, ignited small-scale mud puddle tsunamis.
I then heard the angel's shout, long before her appearance on my bus stop shoreline.
Strange, a surprisingly shrill voice screamed at me.
"Son, get out of there! Now!" Angels save lives, even when they don't sound like angels.
My mud puddle fantasy flaunts a life of its own.
Even at this age, with three score annual scars carved into my knees,
I still repress the urge to roll up my suit pants, discard my

second-hand Italian shoes
(Which incidentally cost more than the family automobile of my youth),
and recommission my mud puddle frigates to battle.
Disappointingly, the engineers in my community dedicated to the seasoned,
have devised strategies to eliminate these tiny lakes
from streets willing to host them.
One scintillating, sunshiny day, as the refreshing aroma of ozone oozed
in the Appalachian air, the seasoned me drove back to a land
of proliferating mud puddles, a university building site.
I left my coughing car, trudged thru Carolina clay, and stood
in the middle of the mother of all mud puddles
striking a Colossus of Rhodes pose.
I paused like Yates at Coole (After the wild swans).
I wondered. I hoped. I dreamed.
My protective angel gone to other puddles
in heavenly pastures.
If, for just a few moments,
I could take off my shoes, roll up my pants,
launch fresh stick boats and resume my admiralty duties,
would my impassioned angel reappear?
If she did, would she sing her shrill aria of love
or would I encounter a white-suited Freudian army?

Free Verse, Spring 2007

Out of Ghetto Experience

Uptown women rarely strayed down the basil scented streets of
my youth.
Surrounded by the sweet sounds of Verdi's sonatas,
stored in a miscast tenement piazza in the New World,
I sunned on a soft, silken carpet of ebony haired, seductive sirens
sired by the fish monger.
When this braided, straw-tufted woman sauntered into my
overstuffed streets
and smiled, flashing straight teeth whiter than a fresh alpine
snow, I gaped.
My mouth stretched wider than at the dentist's command.
This was my first encounter with this sort of lady fair
and my enchantress seemed to have waltzed out
of my English literature books, behind a face radiating like a
Shannon sunset.
The thought of touching her set off internal tremors.
I wondered if even a slight tap on her arm would trigger blotches
on her ashen and impressionable skin.
She couldn't be real. Natural blondes existed in real life?
I recalled celluloid encounters with the breed, in books,
and on Hollywood's screens.
In my youth, they occasionally streaked across my sleep world.
I was smart enough to sense that in my action-filled twelve years.
I'd not seen that exact pigmentation, not in my Brooklyn haunts
anyway.
not on the cement streets and scarred sidewalks of the Pushcart
Ghetto,
with its-stiletto-shoed glow.
A score of years later, throngs of them delighted me
on the necklace of roads ringing drooling Etna in her lava latticed
sky.
As a child, I'd never traveled to Taormina, Toulouse, or

Tipperary.
Never even wandered out of a tiny corner of Brooklyn.
All the guys gawked at the invading Golden- haired uptowner.
Stickball games stopped.
At that moment, a simultaneous sighting of a Martian
would have been dismissed and ignored.
She too, came from another cosmos,
another dimension perhaps, or a parallel universe.
Surely, I never collided with her world, not consciously anyway.
Her smile opened skylights to her mystifying chunk of this planet.
Her soft smile, accented by those ivory teeth,
lured me from my dozen-year ghetto stint.
I accepted her invitation, never to return home.

Oasis Journal, January 2004

Places

Candy Cane Lightposts in Polar Night

My rail car sways and scratches as it grinds out of its urban,
jaundiced tunnel.
It rumbles as it pumps up speed and rhythm,
spreads its clatter while suspended in an ebony sea,
occasionally buffeted by sparks skipping along the tired tracks.
Finally, it chugged toward a snowy Santa-like sunrise,
I streak toward suburbia.
The postcard countryside greets me with a platoon
of candy cane light posts decorated and wrapped in intertwining
knots
of red, white, and blue.
Its wardrobe supplied by cheery folk anticipating holidays.
The splintered posts, sporting ice cycle sideburns,
are crowned with snow-capped, onion shaped babushkas,
similar to those attending to Moscow's squares,
and seem to sparkle in Polar night.

Tapestries Journal, 2003

Lakely Imposters

Wrinkled lake it's been two wars and
a score of rainy seasons since I tattooed your murky neck
with my high topped, circular labeled sneaks.
Today's fancy check marked sneaks, alien lithographs then.
Now, they are more familiar than toads to you.
Time to stretch, time to exercise, time to renew an old friendship.
My step is labored, more strained today.
You too old friend.
Too bad you've blemished.
Your oaken dock is missing wooden teeth. Ruptured.
Your blacktop track is overrun with Martian like canals.
That can't be!
Can't be my face reflecting in you.
No children whirring 'round in all directions now.
No, "Daddy, can we go for pizza?"
No, "Daddy, I want ice cream."
No songs for me this dawn.
Another population of geese prowl.
Their descendants still snort, still grovel, and still beg.
I lumber around your jellied, pitch banks in a choppy, elliptic orbit.
Plodding now. My trek takes me past knarred, pimpled picnic tables.
Smooth as virgin ice once, weren't they? Weren't we?
A new generation of letters and hearts are scratched in redwood.
Your olive park benches flake like dandruff
exposing your old familiar umber.
Your clangy, rust colored box swing, scratches and groans
sending squirrels scurrying.
A nameless father pushes
with the same enthusiasm that I mail my taxes.
His mind locked in another scene.

I want to shout, "Stop, stupid! Enjoy that child, talk to her, hug her."
I too was a reluctant propeller,
So often I heard the command, "Daddy, don't stop pushing."
Too soon the playground pilot grows, deserts your port.
Too soon the spirited symphony ends, children's play and laughter
referenced under wonderful memories...Recollections.
Too soon the shout, "Daddy!" is no longer meant for you.
"Aaah! Hello again, Mr. Giant Cement Turtle."
Still green and yellow, you haven't changed much.
Why has my song been sung?
You disappoint me. You're so fickle. My three discovered you.
My three fed you, though you refused to eat their gourmet mud stew.
My three rode you to enchanted lands.
Now, you allow imposters to saddle you.
Have you heard of loyalty?
Still, your expression remains smug.

The Ascent (Adelphi University), 1993

Columbus Circle Crooner

His jellied legs skate him onto the Nine Train,
merging with commuters crammed much like canned sardines.
His baggy, dangling pants mop subway stations with each slide step.
His floppy tongue-like, soled shoes collect rodent droppings.
The slick suited, those dragging clumsy pallets,
the book and computer laden, the silver tufted, the diapered of all ages:
shaved heads, dreadlocks, burkas, saris, suits, the turban topped,
silk suited, a virtual global diversity of straphangers shroud the new rider.
That unique Big Apple crowd of people,
woven in place and standing shoulder to shoulder in the city's subway,
these tidy travelers working to remain alone in the midst of that pile of people.
Slowly, but with the anonymity of a kick line, the passengers' necks coil
toward the baronial tones wafting from the ashen haired troubadour.
The underground air shimmers with sounds similar to the lilt of the legendary
King Cole.
"Requests?" The singer asks. A philistine exposes his back and covers his ears
as completely as a winter fig tree. Human silence, followed by subway clangs rule.
The singer snakes thru the subway car, shaking his paltry coin cup
like a baby's rattle. "Thanks," he says to his teenaged benefactor
who discerns art and harmony despite her alien apparel.
Parting, the crooner donates another free song,

collects a carload of smiles, but no silver.
His gilded voice nearly camouflages his clanky, crackling, knee cap
as he hops onto the Central Park, Columbus Circle platform
and blends into its crowds.
The music man glides and coughs his way up the street, escaping that
annoying concerto caused by the grimy odor of raspy city buses.
He stares across the dizzying circle, at a swarm of parkland prowlers
beneath the watchful eye of pigeon covered colossal statues.
The crooner pauses, recharges, and slides back down the subway tube,
ready to repeat his act. *Encore*!

Perigee Poetry Journal, January 2005, Contest winner: Virginia Poetry Society

Hunting for Hemingway

As the footage of my days freeze framed across my mind,
I realized that this time, Pamplona's party raged without me.
Nothing new. Craters caused by chicken pox
cancelled my second grade trip.
A moving van eliminated my high school football debut,
a ballooned ankle my anticipated championship hoops season.
Now, a personal economy grounded me from this latest,
"Run with the Bulls."
At the *San Fermin* festival, no reserved will call tickets stored for
me.
Doffed images from rectangular, wide screens brazenly tantalized.
Pallid photographs teased, like rolling yarn extending its wooly
tongue
toward anxious felines.
I recalled my first Pamplona festival, retraced my first steps in
medieval Spain.
That terrain, clad in a crimson and white blanket of effervescence,
sporting head bobbing, neck jerking music and endless upbeat
melodies.
Celebrants from 3 to 103 hung out, diapers too, for all generations.
The sun never slumbered in that original <u>Sun also Rises</u> set.
Hemingway's haunts still seduce.
Scribes dream of literary infusions from the spirit of Papa as they
wait
their dawn appointment with the *corrita de toros*.
Runners pack in behind a human barricade of *polizia*.
Faces tighten, eyes twitch, legs pump, and sweat drains.
Diverse tongues, a multiplicity of skin tones silently scream
as they anticipate the rocket blast releasing single minded bulls.
A red and white soufflé of people surround.
The scent of red wafts thru the soggy air.
The defiant, the brave, the tentative sprinters

challenge doom as tons of rage pound the pavement.
My internal seismograph senses the ruffling of the human heart, much like firecracker sounds that pierce a frightened dog's instincts.
Makeshift planking channels both two and four legged runners.
Cheering observers attach to the sheltered side of fences.
The reasoned and the enraged all share the same wooden chute and route.
Blast! Some sprinters seem to surface under my legs.
No time to stop, soothe, or socialize. Just vault over them.
This is an everyone for himself scenario, an honest depiction of life itself.
I scour my slice of the skies and offer my most sincere prayers, promises, and penances.
Arena aprons finally appear, terrified shrieks of "Toro" slice up from the rear.
A narrow tunnel miraculously appears, sanctioning this runner into the
surreal safety of the near empty bullring.
Not for long.
Toro hurtled past, dusting me on his mad scamper to the corral.
Several espressos later, celebrity was conferred,
"Hey Yank, bravo! You made it!"
I droop my head and acknowledge my literary deity by bowing my head
at Hemingway's bust smirking down at me.

Riversedge Literary Journal, (University of Texas, Pan-American, Spring, 2006

Rainy Days And Distant Muted Moments

Muted voices in the distance squawk with the delight of children
romping in turbulent, heart-shaped pools.
Heavy downpours from an irate sky, force adults to cover,
yet seem to squeeze children out of resort rooms into the
outdoors.
They dive, they splash, they sprint into and out of cascading
pools.
They scurry from swimming pools to ocean.
Edgy birds now hop from resort tower to resort tower.
A combined sonata played by chirping birds
and surfing kids filters thru raindrops.
Busy gray clouds move out, only to be replaced by carbon clouds.
Cheerful children's voices now drown out surf, birds, and the
hammering of relentless rain.

Shemom, Winter, 2010

Outdoor Sunday Service

I'd heard rumors that shrines such as these thrived.
This devotion, this cult of Sunday worship must have been camouflaged
before I moved to a home ,embracing the emerald mound named "The Ninth Hole."
There, on Sundays, long before more traditional worshippers arise,
a flock assembles, gathers in slow motion while clutching caffeine offerings.
Unified, with assorted respectful hats draping an army of hairless heads,
This band of devotees drifts in simultaneously with the sun's deliberate debut.
Men, and a handful of women, sporting somewhat similar cassocks,
whisper and join the processional ceremony, yet remain alone in thought.
They wait for their choirmaster to signal the start of their special
Sunday services, all scheduled to begin at different times.
While hanging 'round, they look beseechingly at the belching, shamrock shaped, ebony tinted clouds nesting above their sacred golfer soil.
They nod in greeting the rest of their sporting congregation,
sharing signs of peace. Behind quivering and disparate lips,
repeat their personal chants and imprecations.
One by one, they saunter to the main mount, stand there,
and meditate while awaiting the starter's signal and blessing.
After that, devotees launch their small spheres toward the distant, flag covered mount.
Each aficionado carries his interactive prayer book, a dwarf pencil,
and prepares for the gospel according to par.
After scaling the neatly shaven, flag occupied hill,

some genuflect beneath the restless and flapping banner.
Reaching into seemly endless pockets,
the worshippers delicately deposit silver donations
atop the smooth shaven, crew cut like grasses, only to reclaim
the coin after tapping the tiny ball in a hole seconds later.
Once the ball rolls into its interim home beneath its flag,
the disciples bow to the flapping flag god,
to fellow followers, dutifully scrub and polish their shiny staffs,
then record their latest numerical litany into their Par Prayer
Book.

Zillah Journal, Spring, 2005

Hardhats Draping the Park

A pack of gashed hardhats: yellow, green, purple, white,
faded and frayed by mounds of mortar, all shielding diverse heads,
fat faces, jowled, bony, lined, unlined, a multichromatic human mosaic
standing in prayerful attention and occupying dangling cubes
in their hardhat grandstand.
These windowless chiseled catbird seats,
in the midst of local stage door renovations totter and sway,
a league above the scurrying crowd on Main Street of the Western World.
These White Way, work free workers, lean and whistle at every high-skirted parader
and are noticed, but ignored by their sophisticated prey.
Finally, a yelp...
"Right on!" She smiled, "guys!"

Facing the neon sign pessimistically proclaiming,
"Dow Drops,"
their spirits leap with a flurry of smiles emerging.
I suppose these perched men won at some sort of lottery.
And, like lottery winners, they play on and on.

Byline Magazine, April 2001 Free Verse Contest, 3rd Place

Murano's Message

We delighted in our discovery of the wrinkled,
scintillating crystal dove while strolling on the tired, shedding streets.
These walkways clung and hugged the bedrock
implanted in Murano's raging waters,
and supported a tiny city of crystal treasures above.
Like an apparition, a story book store confronted and tantalized,
flaunting a dazzling necklace of fine crystal that sparkled in a shop window.
My anxious feet clawed their path the the water-logged via
on this baronial island for a closer look.
Overrun and occupied by glass blowers,
I sprinted toward the showroom, nearer to this glass Jezebel.
This crystal dove flirted with my eyes, glinting, and glistening.
It must have been designed for the exclusive use of angelic choirs,
sporting its bedazzling and mystical lines.
We returned briefly the St. Mark's Square,
a place occupied by warrior pigeons.
After a hiccup-length pause to satisfy our epicurean appetites,
we returned to our two-faced gondola
determined to transport our translucent dove back home,
across the Atlantic.
Unfortunately, the frozen, faceted bird eloped with another tourist.
As my wobbly, pre espresso steps tracked along the Sarasota shoreline,
an affectionate seashore that generously embraced
and poured out its beauty onto the entire bay,
a most intricate sea shell tickled my curiosity.
Unusual in shape, color, and painted only as the Creator could,
it seemed obvious that manmade colors were not allowed
to tattoo that shell.

I gently placed my right Celtic toe over the newly discovered prize,
and vowed to pick it up after the retreat of the next frothy wave.
Wave spent and done, I raised my protective toe,
and howled when I realized that that bandit wave,
with so little strength left, successfully,
stealthily pirated my shell.
Murano's lesson leapt to mind.
When we find that jewel, that unique treasure,
human or not, don't ponder, don't wait.
Scoop and snare it immediately.

Goose River Anthology, 2007

Dockside Show

Evening's smart light limply hangs
deserted over toothy dock,
yet to realize dawn's unannounced arrival.
Its glow of sixty minutes past, merely a twinkle
over spindly walkway to the sea.
Gray everywhere.
Gray-blue waters, with pigmy sized ivory caps surfing.
Nowhere to splash but to meekly slap swampy shore.
The gray sky stubbornly blocks the patient sun
and grudgingly permits persistent rain drops to slip through.
Grayer, skittish birds everywhere too.
A dozen shrieking seagulls slicing the sky in a "V" flying
formation.
Two playmates swooping, flapping and performing an aerial
ballet
for a mysterious choreographer, a celestial puppeteer,
looping the lower sky, and then splashing.
A squealing gull makes desperate overhead pleas.
The BOSS BIRD, chunky bodied and stick legged commands
Sotto voce.
Light grey freckled and dark grey tailed, the BOSS BIRD proudly
prances
then glares arrogantly, yelping for food.
The BOSS blasts off while a discordant staccato chorus sings.
The paltry, scattered flock follows,
while streams of birds soar toward the grey cloaked island of fire.

Serendipity Journal, Fall, 1997

Nice Airport, French Riviera

I sprawled out in the whirling airport waiting room,
stretched and eager to exit this tangled,
pebbled Eden of crumbled czars.
Spread out in the midst of an aircraft anchorage,
I waited for the boarding call to slingshot me
across Atlantis' moat, to the land of Liberty's lip.

A blue suited, rolling, travel bag brigade marched penguin-footed.
Suddenly, all around, the same striped shoulders,
sporting similar suits,
matching rollers, and sharing a kindred rhythm,
behind a brigade of rolling luggage,
romped and raided the airport wait area.
Surely, they'd all graduated from the same
airline sashay training course.

Flight attendants, pilots, and navigators promenaded lock step.
Multi-national air jockeys, donning identical apparel,
wheeled similar, grumbling carry-ons.
How often is this process repeated?
I wonder if their interminable travels everywhere
really evolve into voyages to nowhere?

Offerings, Fourth Quarter, 1999

Park Playpen

Sunrise. A picture book oasis framed in grainy concrete.
Runners, squandering motion, scrambling like mice in this maze,
wrapped in illusory liberation.
Free to bounce anywhere within the designated slats.
Soul infused knock hockey pucks determined to earn beaded tributes,
stripes, secured by sweat.
Reflections of a turf where evil briefly flourished,
where the damned cloaked themselves in pious vestments
and dared say, "God bless."
Unshaken denizens insist upon challenging these apathetic foot paths.
These thoughts loiter as my hoarsed voiced knees grumble
and awaken the zoo's tenants.
In the thick of a flailing rush, sprints to nowhere,
I sample this village sized fire drill of churning legs gone amuck.
Dawn exercisers, followers of fitness gurus
sporting all sorts of joggers, walkers, a sampling of a multiplicity of styles,
and annual wrinkles, tinted in multiple hues.
Today a solitary language, and a smatter of dialects
echo among bobbing baseball caps.
Mechanical males clank about like oaken Christmas toys,
while more jelly-bellied men labor with lobster-like gait.
Dowdy women flaunt struts that would swell seminary enrollments.
A background of horse-driven carriages,
powered by hefty equines who
commandeered the table at feed time clatter by:
The swift and balletic,
The staccato stepped,
The tall and lean,

The short and chunky.
Even laid back runners with furtive eyes fixed on the setting moon,
plead for inspiration.
People sharing asexual garb assemble without mixing.
Monumental efforts, a parade of perspirers
are all invisibly tethered and leashed.
All vie for real estate tracts on the sunken meadow
surrounded by a mural of slumbering skyscrapers.
Savvy urban pigeons gawk at the panoply of sunrise scramblers
as they boomerang toward playpen's Main Street.
Determined and driven, soaking in human brine,
moist evidence of spirited winners.

Zillah Poetry Joournal, 2002

Porthole to Paris

I shared the ocean sky to Paris with porthole window 23A,
and its plastic, grooved shade, suspended and frozen in place.
It framed my face, lobster claw style.
Together we soared across the foaming Atlantic.
My head rested, nestled in the Oriel's well-rounded bosom.
The shade pressed and bound tightly, just me and 23A.
Occasionally, this jittery, impromptu pillow jarred,
and momentarily scrambled heaven's door.
Awakened, I flexed my neck as gracefully as a mechanical dinosaur.
Poplar tree shaped clouds protected smaller, snow coned sister clouds
and pinched up toward my soaring, populated pencil
hanging and dangling in the heavens.
Free agent sheer and surreal clouds swaggered
in a failed attempt to mask the reliable sun.
Acrylic skies, snaky waterways and a wisp of grey,
willowy smoke signaled the twin arrivals
of twilight and *terra firma*.
The airliner's fin, tattooed with an American flag tipped,
then bowed to earth and sky.
Star splashed wings shimmered as engine three hissed
like a raging Florida rattler.
Unseen cosmic lips blew velvety clouds
that crossed our celestial horizon.
A mirage of fools' diamonds shimmered below.
A touchable siphoning vacuum sapped, straitjacketed my soul.
Sweat drained in my restricted echo chamber.
I eased out of my porthole, swamped by swells of separation.
My heart hungered and missed my exclusive concerto,

my Celtic belle, and the branches of my genetic tree.
I sat up. Still. Suspended, yet moving mercurially.
Me, my porthole, and an insatiable panorama of God's infinity.

Hiking Thru Herculaneum

I strolled with my tour guide and squeaky kneed vacationers.
We heard talk of history's imprimatur tattooed
to the ground on which we walked.
We saw plaster outlines of people like us, with loves,
anticipations, visions, and families blanketed by Hell's fiery curse,
suddenly covered in debris, dust, and pumice.
The last frenetic moments of their lives freeze framed
by an enraged volcano belching demise and boiling drool.
Despite the finality of the setting, it still felt like
I'd somehow parachuted onto the midst of a horrifying,
blood-curdling fairy tale.
I recalled Pliny the Younger's description of Herculaneum's
Doomsday Hours.
He shuddered when describing ominous clouds hunting down
victims,
the eradication of any trace or speck of light, delivering a
blackness more pronounced that that of a New York subway tunnel.
He spoke of blinded babies, children, and adults wailing
when a scintillating day turned into a ghoulish dreary night.
He lamented losing touch with scrambling loved ones on the exit
route,
especially his uncle, the Elder Pliny.
Goose pimples stamped my arms as the events of two millennia
past
came home to me on that sweaty, foul smelling Mediterranean
afternoon.
Now, as I looked at that ancient holocaust
and its terrorized timeless faces,
I sensed their despair, their panic, and desperate prayers
to a hegemony of indifferent gods.
All to no avail.

My travel thru time lost its entertainment and educational value.
The grim reality of callous history began to sicken me.
I poured water on my head, ran a dry towel across my face,
then lumbered like a drowsy St. Bernard pup,
right out of that sacred burial ground.
Lacking the curiosity of Lot's wife, I refused to look back.
I scampered away seeking a fast track out,
while vowing never to return.

Riversedge Literary Journal (University Of Texas, Pan-American, Spring, 2010)

Brooklyn Bridge

I lounged next to the tick tac toe lined window of the tired hotel,
and settled under the rippling shadow of the Brooklyn Bridge.
Sunrise laborers appeared thru my wrinkled and scrunched perch.
Awakened by the tickle of an impromptu breeze
that slithered around the edges of the hearty brick buildings,
while husky shouting joined whistling voices.
I sat speechless as this army of laborers hauled, piled and stacked.
The workers were escorted by as parade of fork lifts
meandering thru a Hong Kong type traffic jam.
I'd never seen so many of these fork shaped machines
in one place as they navigated over surviving colonial
cobblestone.
Patient trucks sat open mouthed as ice boxed fish were gently
stuffed in their gut by toothy forklifts.
Fishmongers' operatic commands and echoing laughter thundered
all around New York's sunrise splashed harbor.
Fiery workers with crimson lined, calloused hands,
peeled, scaled,and loaded fish for a hungry nation.
Sounds blanketed sounds, shouts suppressed more timid yelps,
as a brigade of American flags moved under, then climbed above
toward the bridge freckled by time and salt.
After several hours of bristle, bustle, worker chants,
the satiated trucks took their ocean booty onto the pot holed
roads,
as they readied deliveries to elegant eateries.
Capped joggers lumbered above on the wiry, pencil lined paths.
Forklifts returned to their stables as their boisterous jockeys
washed, changed clothing, tasted a tad of *vino* from straw coated
Sicilian bottles, and then followed their fish across the crusty
bridge.
This pimpled carroty, rusted expanse, framed by glittering webs,
outstretched its weary and ruddy tentacles with balletic flair,

while its footings were embraced and massaged by its friendly
river.
Hoarse voiced pavement sweepers scrubbed, rubbed, and
brushed the bridge hoping to dress her for a new day.
For generations, this bridge delivered to and for America.
This seasoned steel link continues to connect States with its unique
form of room service, and to shroud its passionate colony
of fishmongers nestled under its toes.
What were those fools thinking? Did they really think that
their mass murder of this disparate tribe of Americans
would extinguish this spirit, this energy, this drive,
and this patch quilt of invincible souls?
Spirited men with relief mapped hands defiantly snub their noses at thugs
targeting them for terrorism. One squint, one peek out of my
cracked hotel room window dispels that heresy that these people flinch.
The oversized sized old glory cockily flaps in their face of zealots.

Daddy Daze

Swing Set

I squeak.
Old age attacks my arthritic, metal joints.
My voice grindy, scratchy, hoarse.
I could use a few swigs of three in one oil.
Ironic...my face peels.
Blotches...pale...
Too many years.
Too much sun.
Piles of Long Island snows.
Salty sea breath from my neighbor,
the hovering, mammoth Atlantic monster.
Despite his stormy nature, his extortion,
I've had happy days spent with tiny friends.
Up...Down...
They piloted me thru friendly, earthbound skies.
Together, we breezed with their boundless, youthful dreams.
I don't hear children anymore.
I can't remember exactly when the chatter ended
and the laughter stopped.
I can barely recall the sweet sounds of children giggling.
Silence always now.
All grown.
I see them occasionally, too big for me now, almost adults.
They fail to return my stare, it's like I don't exist.
Unrequited.
Peter are you still angry about the five stitches?
You came crashing into me.
Mary, I loved watching you cartwheel.
I cried with you when you chipped your tooth on my slide.
Jon, my tiny swing was not designed to soar well above
my broad barred shoulders.
I'm sure that your buddy basketball triggered you

to skin your knees much worse than my swing.
The growing kids splash past me, soak me after each pool dip.
They sprint by me, chasing uncooperative, defiant basketballs.
They don't stop in anymore.
Graduation day, that's the last time I got any attention.
Not that "Family" really cared about me.
Showtime! They don't want their guests looking at
a shoddy, freckled me.
Before their party, "Family" brushed me with gaudy,
bright color and left me alone to dry.

The Ascent (Adelphi University), Spring, 1993

A Father's Advice to Daughters

Make sure your prince believes you're the best,
even if you have occasional doubts about it.
Make sure he understands the depth and breadth of your fire,
he reads your passion for life and discovery,
he recognizes your need to feed the hungry, even if
unappreciated.
Make sure he respects your unique appetite for knowledge,
pleasantly skates around the piles of books pyramiding in your
room.
And, as a modern soul sister of Duse and Montessori, make sure
he accepts your need to unravel obscure byways, open
mystifying doors, and explore rusty attic boxes.
March those extra miles, probe the exotic and mysterious,
continue toppling unique stones, defying possible dangers
lurking all 'round, in the hope of trapping a possible insight
and shining the spotlight of your imagination on it.
Make sure the potential prince respects your rage to discover
and finds your springtime stubbornness refreshing.
Be sure that he won't rage when you fail and disappoint, as we all
do.
Be careful that he walks with you when you want,
but realizes that there are times that you need to take your shoes
off
and tiptoe across the stony beach alone, as its scruffy,
sandy beard massages your feet.
Be sure he allows you the space to grow and breathe,
genius needs these ingredients to fully blossom.
And, at your time of solitude, of tension, of chilling sweat,
be sure he's in the wings ready to motivate, encourage, and
shelter.
Make sure he allows you the time to sip and savor your
cappuccino

and if you stubbornly make a flippant remark to him, he laughs it off.
If you never learned to ride a bicycle, dive from the high board, drive a race car, or compose sonatas,
make sure he encourages and patiently guides you along,
even rolls out his red carpet to support your success.
If he proves tender in such matters,
how much more tender will he be in matters of the heart?
Make certain that he allows you to scrape your knees,
splinter your hands, experience minor scratches, bumps, and bruises
when you walk in the bramble and bushes in your dogged hunt for knowledge and completion.
Make sure that while he showers you with affection,
and he doesn't drown you with demands.
Make sure that when the tainted backwash of
disappointment splashes the shorelines of your soul,
he serves as your lifeguard to broad shoulder you to sanctuary.
And, when you apply a brake to your explorations,
make sure he welcomes you with a parade in his heart.

Riversedge Literary Journal (U Of Texas Pan/American) Spring, 2006

Theme Park Daddy

I'm not really good at this, nor do I plan to be.
Don't ask me to adjust.
The early eviction from my fleeced Daddy nest
boils my blood.
I enviously watch young vacationers walking hand-in-hand
with floppy-legged, wailing children screeching and spewing
their litany of complaints.
The familiar chant, from unfamiliar voices penetrates my ears.
The alien Pop is bombarded, "Dad when's dinner?"
The father glares down at the boss child, and calmly answers.
"It's at five son. We have a half hour," he says,
and tries to extinguish hunger with a loud hug.
Too bad that hemorrhage of hugs fails to bear hug
the clock's unrelenting and hasty arms.
Time flows as freely as the morning tide pounding the beach,
nothing slows it.
Déjà vu drapes me.
You see, I savored my daddy time.
I reveled in the pretentious silence of gymnastic meets.
The deafening cheers of hoop contests enlivened me,
while the word play at little league games amused me.
The unplanned, yet real time, trumpet solos at elementary
school concerts, meet-the-teacher nights, ice cream, coffees, teas,
pizza after recitals, and a potpourri of other school related rituals
charmed me, all misty memories now.
That's all there is to Daddyhood.
You're soon promoted to Pop, Poppy, or Granddad.
My inner Dad still wonders why this bandit,
masqueraded in the robes of time,
has fast forwarded this part of my life,
swiftly hijacked these magnificent moments,
so coldly, so quickly, so effectively, and with such finality.

So, theme park Dad, frolic with your lads and lassies while you can,
for in an earthly moment, indistinguishable as it were,
the stage door of youth will slam, and boot you from its pedestal.
You'll wake up jilted by young adulthood,
exiled to a canyon of soppy reminisces, while replacement Dad teams
prance on your former field of fatherhood.

Free Verse Literary Journal, #95, 2008

Rusted Rim

Shedding. Bits of orange flakes, ritzy nylon lingerie,
silky netting once cloaked my droopy hoop rim.
Twenty hours a day, the center of attention.
Spoiled. Hugged. Needed.
The first adjustable backboard in the hood.
My little friends dangled like playful spiders,
reduced me to seven feet, dunked, and drained me.
Those were my glory days,
sunrise to sunset basketball marathons.
My tiny freckle-nosed gymnast never jammed balls down my throat.
Her rumba reserved for me only.
She presented me a sneak preview of future arena dances.
Little brothers bopped to a different rhythm.
They bounced the ball between their broomstick legs,
behind their backs too, and jarred me by hurling shots.
All sorts of slams buffeted me from every direction.
Summertime air shimmered with swishing sounds.
Dad served icy soda to bands of kids jousting with me.
In fall, acorns never dared to dot my apron.
They were swept away pronto by my brigade of loitering pals.
Wintry snows disappeared from my view
long before state plows scratched my neighboring streets.
Then, things changed around here, changed a lot.
It all began after they started ramming the rod into my throat
and managed to raise me to full height.
I felt ten feet tall. My nets lasted longer, more games played elsewhere,
against wimpy, indoor, pampered glass backboards.
Gleamy eyed Big Little Guy, Mr. Esquire now,
transported his game to another court.
The leather he handles today is a busy briefcase

weighted with court orders and demands.
Little Guy took his straw locks to the Capital Centre
where national announcers yelped, "Gotta love the little guy!"
Spotted nose unleashed her cheery ballet in front of thousands,
beneath Big Apple's upper crust backboard glass at Madison's
Garden.
I saw her first!
My greatest humiliation came when Dad huffed up to his
stepladder's
top rung to exorcise an evil nest of interloping bees camped in my
neck.
A lopsided, airless ball now lounges below me.
A sign of the times. A reminder. Metallic acne in my rusting years,
no one bothers to sweep pesky acorns off my paunch anymore.
Occasionally, Dad comes out, gives me a wrinkled brow look,
as if he's watching ghosts of games past,
where games never ended. Then, he rubs his silver beard,
takes some lame shots, and shuffles back into the house,
lonely as a fish stranded on a dry sandbar,
without an ocean in sight.

Goose River Anthology, 2006

Playing Catch With Kids

I saw them soft tossing the cowhide baseball thru the swarthy
summer twilight and swallowed the same ball field dust that
prodded
my numerous, cleansing coughs during my hirsute days.
A dad and his boy lobbing a loop arched ball in a sort of lazy,
slow motion while playing catch.
The catch game has always been more than fathers and sons to
me.
Still, I hoped that that unidentified dad savored and relished
those special seconds.
You see, I did it first, countless sunsets past.
At the unfolding scent of spring, as tan grasses splashed green,
and flowers prepared for spring debuts,
I remember my three children marching me out for springtime
catches.
A reluctant fool, I never realized how rare and prized
those moments would soon become. I revel at the memories
of tossing a baseball to my daughter and sons as it scraped thru
thick and murky August skies.
Each throw, every soft toss, carried dreams along those cowhide
seams.
They were images of ball field glory, of fame, of adoring fans,
and our select circle laced by love and family.
When enthusiasts occasionally tried to interlope,
to bore into "our" game, our faces took on the blush of ripe
tomatoes.
It was "our thing" as much as crime belonged to mobsters.
Those days, those madcap minutes of wonder,
have nearly deserted my landscape of imagination.
Glorious hours filed away with the soot of decayed days.
Those moments of baseball juggling,
the playful derision and laughter after a dropped ball,

along with the praise afforded dexterity
with leather covered hands forever faded.
Mystery man, anonymous, grumbling father
pitching to your son, freeze those moments,
simmer and bind them about your being.
Soon, they'll discourteously desert you too.
The hours are merciless and soft tosses are eventually replaced
by long distance notes, twits, twitters and calls as family circles
unravel and eventually detach themselves into a great, white
silence.

Zillah Poetry Journal, Winter 2002

Last Game

The jump shot swishes, barely brushing the rim.
Scoreboard ticks and registers two more.
Is that all there is? He wonders.
The senior player, swarmed by toothy teammates,
lopes toward the soppy bench and,
remains speechless in the mouth of mayhem.
A dozen pimpled backs stand:
two dozen hands clap with the voice of one.
The fuzzy faced freshman runs
onto the parquet floor for his debut.
After a round of chest bumps and high fives,
the scarecrow haired player looks at the game clock and squints.
Eyes fixed; he loiters, biting down on dry lips.
He hangs his drooling jacket over freckled shoulders,
and sits droopy headed.
A few moments later, he scans the peeling crowd
and stands dazzled by undulating fingers of light,
so different from his cratered, tree crowded backyard home court.
Searching beyond shapes and shadows,
he focuses on his most enduring fan.
The boy winks.
Suddenly, he's back to kerosene winters, dank gymnasia,
decorated with dangling ropes,
his first behind the back dribble,
his opponent and best pal falling
while writhing in laughter and,
a toothy faced, well-postured black beard winking,
a twinkle in his look.
They'd not planned for his hoop ball curtain to fall
with such finality. There was no warning and no encore.
The game would never end,
so thought the boy and his dad.

Sporting a soft, fuzzy chin,
the boy swaggers off the mirrored basketball court.
With moodiness trickling from his soul,
he speaks thru a raspy voice.
"Pop," he says with raised brow, "for most of my life,
from my eighth birthday to my twenty-first year,
I've suited for this game. Is that all there is?"
His biggest fan resorts to tip toes and plants a kiss
on his boy's dripping cheek.
Then, the player wipes off the mix of sweat and tears,
arm draped around a slumping, steely bearded father.

Goose River Anthology, 2009

What Is It?

She opened the car doors and children spilled out, and scrambled,
following commands from some unseen conductor.
They scattered in all directions,
rolling over and over like primitive lawnmowers.
Just moments earlier, these youngsters had settled in a fantasy world,
prompted by the massaging effects of the car ride.
Now, the visit to the green carpeted arboretum fired them,
made them appear like captured mustangs released from a pen into the wilderness.
She wondered, what is it about grasses, trees, and wide open spaces
that inspires children to choose to spin over and over, and then run wildly?

Portals, Spring 2003

Nostalgia

Ghost-Town Garden

My bicycle froze when I confronted the flaking javelin like gate.
This yard had served as an oasis, flaunting carved, linear,
grooved rows of tomato plants, chives, radishes, and broccoli.
It boasted a tidy, yet tangled grape arbor and a stately,
whitewashed religious statue.
Interlopers were unwelcome and violently uprooted from this turf.
The sentinel, a pot marked, broad shouldered fig tree
stripped her winter coat of witch-like tar paper,
and draped nearby plants like an umbrella.
In the far corner, shuffling in the rusted shed, behind claw-like,
quivering fingers, tinkered one of the last surviving veterans of
Verdun.
This scene repeated itself each sticky, sweltering August day.
Today felt different. No hunched tinkerer. No untrampled rows.
No budding plantings. Gone too, the contagious laughter
of countless children's children and their shouts of "Papa!"
All that remained of past reality was the snooty fig tree,
reigning over its kingdom, now overrun by a plague of weeds
and exposing a slaughtered symmetry.
Even the orderly grapes took to expansion, they slinked all over.
The garden looked as disheveled as a hairpiece
caught in a surprise Florida rain shower.
As a humble sign of respect, these marauding weeds, groveling grapes,
and tail chasing dogs left an unsullied path in front of the statue.

Riversedge, Spring, 2006

Scraps of Life

I stretch back, wrapped like a mummy as this jetliner
slashes and shimmies through ebony clouds
on its way to my tropical future.
Just a *demitasse* ago, I'd taken my last steps in my *mamma's* home.
The riot of colors remained,
but rivers of family photographs vanished and,
although the contour remained the same,
my mother's flaking home felt like an alien house.
Gone forever her contagious laughter.
Gone forever the tantalizing aromas of secret sauces
wafting through its dollhouse rooms.
Today's former relatives seem as closely related to me
as the fellow straphangers I'd just abandoned on the urban
subway.
A smog of shame, however, smeared the relations and
rendered them like unmade beds.
As seamlessly as mom's heart bonded the family,
it dissolved with her paralyzed pulse.
Her intense love blinded me to our flawed family tree.
No doubt she would loathe today's seemingly polite
estrangement.
My memory leaks past scenes through its landscape of life's clips.
I remember mother's gnarled hands comforting
the boy me through three bouts of pneumonia.
In leaner times,
I remember that same woman giving me her last morsel of food.
I remember that daughter of *Dante* introducing me to *poesia*.
I complained to my children that scavengers
swallowed all scraps and remnants of her life
at the start of her final sleep.
I complained about the ant-like army of pretentious societal
darlings,

God fearing blood, but not soul mates.
Surely, *Mamma* witnessed thru teary and tired eyelids
those slobbering occupiers collecting and stripping my memories
from walls and drawers.
No surprise in this society fueled by illusion.
I'd seen sinners sanctified before.
Brandishing the refreshing wisdom of youth,
my son said, "Dad, let go. She lives in your words."

Silly Return

A slim, scintillating student says,
"It's on the third floor of Collegiate Hall."
I huff toward that third tier and notice the same, tired
pre-digital clock pasted sideways atop the cinder block wall.
This same, lazy timepiece kept me waiting for my spring love
to exit 313's evening French class, at the noontime of my life.

Tonkin Gulf guns exploded on exotic shores.
The mighty Yanks were still powered by the M&M boys.
Daily, I occupied my box seat niche on the third floor sill,
staring at suburban boredom.
During those stormy times, shy, hesitant charcoal hair
began to emerge on my rosy chin.

I return today, grabbing my weathered, steel wooly chin and
push and bully the weary "NO" door,
choosing to ignore its "YES" door twin.
Old habits, like drops of honey stick.
Despite thirty rainy seasons of growth
those familiar oak trees outside the window and life's clock
reflect one moment.

I struggle to elevate my well fed haunches
onto that old, yet familiar sill.
I now cover up two tiles when I sit.
I see that same cream colored grout trickled dry,
side to side, between tiles.
The same sizzling radiator, showing its pockmarks
of age hisses below the sill.
The same college bell hums and signals
the moment of freedom.
People move frenetically.
I abandon my silly office forever.
This time, my lassie doesn't exit 313.

Serendipity, Fall, 1997

California Soul Food

They splashed in like ivory whispers,
animated American angels surrounded and straddled
between the hotel door's dazed marble cherubs.
These Daughters of the Golden Gate connected to our tour group
melding into our seasoned ranks.
They promenaded patiently, soaking up culture
and absorbing professorial wisdom.
My eyes froze, captivated as these mortal cherubs deliberated
and discussed while slithering past Michelangelo's David.
They stood military style, magnetized and bewitched
before Mona Lisa.
They scrutinized, with wide open mouths the stretching fingers
atop the Sistine chapel.
All the while, they strolled and glided to their own enchanting
symphony of breaths and curves.
I sat surrounded in the shadow of Toulouse Lautrec's ghost
bathing in the magnificence of the Moulin Rouge's latest dancers,
only to be distracted by their identical disarming smiles
and child-like giggles.
These lassies appeared as humble golden poppies,
while they oozed like a rhapsody wafting in on Pacific zephyrs.
These fellow travelers also seemed like a celebration of soul,
an American benediction to illuminate sterile,
ashen, and ancient soils and to splash
their oversupply of blessings onto tired terrain.
Lumbering, square shaped prowlers squeezed, whistled, flirted.
This bounce, this verve, this rhythm, this spontaneity
alien to them as watermelon on lobster,
miscast vibrancy in a sea of staid sobriety.
These blossoming valley girls exuded a fragrance, a distilled
draft which refreshed the careworn Continental canvas.
These Californians, gone forever now,

so I now package my vision in word links and chains,
scrambling to cover up the vacuum triggered by this drain
of effervescence.
Despite the fading scent of bouquets and that boundless
emptiness
dripping into my days,
I realize that as I rewind my life that all the treasures
I saw locked in the Louvre,
all the sculpture scintillating the Accademia,
and all gold plate framing the Vatican,
failed to ignite my spirit as well as these free spirited
little fire storms, these California coeds.
Eureka and ciao belle!

Serendipity Poetry Journal, Fall, 1998

Canvas Covered Chevy

Every day as I lumbered on squawking rails
to work in the concrete tower,
thru tear glazed windows, I paused a second and snapped a mental photo
of a '57 Chevy blanketed by a faded and tattered brown canvas cover.
Each morning at the same frame in life's film,
tissues absorbed moisture from the shorelines of my eyes,
so, I vowed to visit the old car.
One dawn, headlines on the newspaper left on my seat screamed:
"U.S. TO ESTABLISH RELATIONS WITH VIETNAM."
I walked off that groaning train,
strolled past the billboard that camouflaged my first kiss,
clutched an aging oak tree,
and ran my grainy fingers over the carving
of a misshapen heart on near its trunk.
I kicked chunks of asphalt off the street that in its prime
embroidered starry scars on each of my knees.
Finally, Rico's house stared me down.
It appeared unchanged, despite scores of winter snows.
The neighborhood melancholy.
The street, once lined with spindly legged ballplayers,
now dotted with dead cars, became an automobile graveyard
sporting cars, all stripped, without hearts or parts.
Wrinkled, tired, pancake shaped tires
stretched on fractured curbs, these streets
mysteriously cratered like Etna's droppings,
windowless houses flourished, like toothless hockey players.
Rico's place, framed by a beaming, shiny silver fence,
shrouded in ageless crimson bricks, sat,
seemingly quarantined,
an oasis in an urban wasteland.

The front door of the brick house moaned and groaned open.
Behind pop bottle glasses, clinging to narrow nostrils,
a map faced woman with a ivory pony tail feebly whispered.
"Petey, it's you. I don't believe it!"
Straining to look, she added, "Rico isn't home you know.
He'll be home soon. He's somewhere out West.
I'm still waiting, but...Hold on!
I remember now.
Come in, and have an egg cream.
Your favorite."

Enrico's Tree

I stumbled mid-stride past Enrico's tree,
chasing a defiant squirrel.
I hardly recognized the scarred red maple tree
under its cathedral ceiling of boughs.
I named her Red.
A half dozen bouffants blanketed her branches
since our last encounter.
Now mature, Red stood tall,
pushing toward power lines and closer to clouds.
Limbs rose, outstretched, saluting God's sky.
Less than a decade past, she bowed without dignity,
on her prayer rug of tattered blue grass,
and bent feebly, trembling in the wind with leaves
kissing soil while branch elbows pierced turf.
She hung hunched, seemingly too frail to live on.
Defeated. Beaten. Battered.
Assaulted and hammered by the bullying,
huffing Atlantic hurricane.
Attacker satiated, leaving his drool of destroyed homes,
property, and lives.
I approached with pal, Enrico.
I raised Red upright. She snapped back. Defied me.
The listless tree rubber banded herself
down toward the grass,
limbs and branches followed in spastic fits.
The sandpaper like hands of near century old Enrico
then lifted, cradled, and massaged.
He too hunched. He too victimized by so many seasons
of solitary darkness, weighed down by countless tons
of coal miner millstones from Pennsylvania's mines.
Still, this descendent of the Dolomites
yanked hapless Red toward his canal riddled and pocked face,

then wrapped the small, feeble tree in his trembling, rutted arms.
Enrico trawled, stretched, and pried
groaning to straighten Red,
despite her stubbornness and protestations.
Much like the fish net seamstress, he positioned Red in a canvas blanket,
tied her in taught cord and added string bandages to patch wounds.
Red looked like a curious circus tent without a showtime,
lines and ropes tethered in a trinacria of symmetry.
Ironic, today Red poses tall and muscular.
Her physician sleeps below in eternity,
basking in Red's revival and triumph.

Melting Trees Review, Fall, 1996

Picture Frame, Frozen in Time

I stooped over to scoop socks out of the drawer.
There, cuddled in a scattered assortment of socks,
I felt something glassy brush my hand.
As I slowly slipped it out from its sock sleeve,
a smudged frame bubbling with a spray of memories
touched me.
My three babies stared at me.
It was our last family portrait before the inevitable and
natural changes promoted by maturity on Father Time's Freeway.
For a moment, I returned to last century's calendar
and to my fleeting days of youth, recognizing the sculpted faces
of my babies, now as mature as the me proudly posing in that
photo.
I recalled those enchanted smiles.
All of those babies have their own babies.
The familiar smiles are still there.
They just make cameo appearances nowadays.
Smiley faces are rarely spawned by Dad any longer.
Like a bicycle tire's slow leak, it all faded undetected.
There wasn't warning, not even a hissing sound to prepare me.
Where had our privately shared songs gone?
"Day is Done" only plays in my mind now.
Our unique pranks and jokes are barely remembered today.
Sure, they exist, but it seems only in Dad's reveries.
I ran the back of my hand across my eyes,
snatched a tissue, scrubbed some defiant prints off
the fairy tale family, then turned the tissue over
to wipe renegade and uninvited moisture from my eyes.

Free Verse, Issue 99/100, 2009

Downsizing

Now that the music melts into images of past landscapes,
a sense of timelessness shrouds me.
My seemingly endless night expires,
and the band slowly shreds eternally, with its
human shrapnel sprinkled across latitudes.
Even without our familiar chorus,
I can't help humming its haunting melodies.
I sit here, held hostage by my pad and pencil,
alone and isolated in a roomful of friends,
replaying my madrigal in the meadows of my mind
and reliving: her upbeat cantata,
her slight frowns,
her harsh stares,
her sassy smiles,
her playful ball games,
her air shimmering sprints,
her reckless plunge into work,
her *joie de vivre*,
and, her flavored tears which I gladly swabbed
to bandage her delicate bleeding spirit.
We splashed simultaneously on the same document pool.
She captained the sleek, modern schooner.
I navigated the careworn, chubby rowboat.
And, occasionally when our mismatched oars crossed,
she, with keyboard tantalizing fingers,
gently guided and tugged me thru wondrous waters,
bleakness too.
With the band's dismantling, I snatch my penned chisel
and dig elsewhere for deposits of spontaneity.
Perhaps, like Chekhov, I resurrected my lost childhood
in her youthful verve. No matter.
This poet, a disloyal parasite

collects samples and supplies of excitement and creativity
that he fails to generate. Of course, she'd be replaced.
So, much like Diogenes, I'm compelled to search,
in my never-ending push to secure a charismatic clone.
On some soulful day, this seasoned professor will point
to the big screen at a nameless college and say,
"I knew her once, for a few bedazzling moments,
we sailed the same stream.
She splashed my soul with her sunshiny song.
The girl can dance too, but,
I'll bet that she still can't hit the curve ball."

Biffs' Quarterly, Spring, 2002

Time Out

I travel the silver lapstrake daily.
Each morning, the 7:37 scratches, grinds, and slithers its way
toward the land of populated peaks, and leather lined towers,
always pausing at your unscheduled station, without masters.
It salutes your junction with its raspy scream,
and charcoal smoke puff, his way of paying homage.
I see you building, empty frail, gaunt.
You once looked like Superman's Daily Planet nest.
There you stand. Now, shabby queen without domain.
Leader without disciples. Ship without mates.
Still lofty...Still arrogant...Still speechless.
A Cyclops sized hole is gouged into your main spire,
a colossal MADE IN USA clock once rattled and rumbled
in your bosom, its hands dictated the course of lives.
Nestled in its oval balcony, it strutted.
Now, your ticking eyeball surgically removed,
gauche grooves, scars, and graffiti artists claim you as billboard.
You stand alone, deserted, and silenced.
Abandoned, you who once fed thousands of families,
you the enabler, the jobber who provided US War Bonds
that pried open ivied college doors for the masses.
You, once major world-wide distributor of watches.
Thanks to the sweat of teeming humanity
in your crankcase,
you helped carry your workers
thru two great wars.
You, so faithful.
There you sit, silenced.
Ironic, suicidal,
a victim of your own precious hands of time.
You, once housed the Queen of Clocks,
your yard now owned and operated

by last century's enemies.
Your dominion is now an apron of rusted mufflers,
and grainy, limp rubber tires.
Topless, doorless, stripped automobiles,
skeletons of their once proud bodies,
covered and surrounded
by urine stained mattresses.

Offerings Poetry Quarterly, Third Quarter, 1995

Isn't It Weird?

Isn't it weird?
One can thrive in a paradise,
and never know it until it's totally vanished?
Disappeared, almost as if that Cloud Nine never existed,
replete with its fun, friendships, friends, family.
It morphed into just fading memories.
Too bad that appreciation
can't be taught as easily
as simple addition.

Just a Walk in the Park

It was supposed to be just a walk in the park,
a cameo visit to the capital of the world,
stretching and rubber banding up the nighttime Lincoln Memorial
behind bands of bamboo legged teenagers
on parent subsidized bus tours.
Someone in my troupe suggested our visiting the Vietnam
Memorial.
I strolled casually, neatly in line behind a patch quilt of tourists
listening to their muted rivers of clattering over pavement
echoing through dense Potomac air.
Names, thousands of names.
Lives, thousands of lives.
Loved ones, thousands of loved ones,
engraved into that outstretched tombstone of lists.
Flickering candles highlighting photos of pocked faces, trinkets,
prayers strewn along the roll call of victims,
all hugging this capital city altar fueled by sacrificial blood of
youth.
A few staccato steps later, my emotions cooled
as I admired spirited sculptures of American men and women
serving and sacrificing in that wasteland of saturated rice patties.
Books sat decaying under glass, brimming with yellowed pages
embracing a litany of lives, much like what must exist at Heaven's
Gate.
I stumbled upon the 1975 edition,
and searched a name in that random year.
My knees suddenly betrayed me and buckled,
while my eyes simultaneously dimmed and dampened
when the name bulged out of the discolored,
washed out pages.
I pawed my way to a nearby bench
and thought about one of my closest college chums.

His personality was like an unkempt bed,
yet his heart was like a baker's confection.
We shared the rhythm of our era, much of the rhythm anyway.
Lieutenant Alberto never had a chance.
I tried to bathe the moment in prayer.
Prayer boycotted me.
All that was left of that flamboyant barrister and friend
were fond memories of nubile females and '56 Fords and
'57 Chevies.

Friends Anthology, 2005

The Face of Courage

I clearly saw the face of courage, in her resolute eyes,
and her set jaw. I felt shrouded by humility, irony,
and surprise.
Surprised, since I'd been teased by glimpses oozing from this
caretaker of the confused, yet,
I'd never recognized it.
Humbled, because with all the rainy seasons
that buffeted my life, my recognition of humanity's rare stepchild,
colossal courage,
should have appeared sooner, especially ironic
since we'd just walked on pavement once shadowed by Rhodes'
Colossus.
Oh sure, I'd known Congressional Medal of Honor
winners, and I'd recognized their heroics.
Yes, there were those misguided folk who actually thought me
courageous after my surviving random sprays of bullets,
or even my scratch free run with Pamplona's half ton bulls.
Not so...
I had no idea that the leaded salvoes were headed my way.
Pure survival instinct dragged my clawing, scrambling body to
safety.
As for those bulls, sure they were life threatening.
Sure my racing blood cascaded thru stressed veins
in panic.
Sure, I survived the sprint.
Fact remained that once I stood trapped
in those narrow Spanish streets,
there was no escape hatch anyway.
I'd dashed into the point of no return.
If some stray rescue helicopter had suddenly hovered over those
Pamplona streets and lowered
a hanging basket, I would have somersaulted into its first class

section. After hiking on the untidy site of the ancient wonder, the Temple Artemus,
after clattering over tired bricks buried in the lava coated streets of Pompeii, after cruising the muscular Mediterranean Ocean, it came to me. An epiphany.
She stood before me every day on our exotic tour of
Circe's Courtyard.
She walked. She talked.
This woman obviously victimized by an
unwelcome affliction, faced it, head on.
Her glowing face masked all pain, pain that would have driven others to rest homes and isolation.
We sat beside a dried, spent river bed,
sapped of moisture and energy.
The lingering haze of Mount Vesuvious blanketed us.
While I swatted gnats, she tackled the behemoth of Parkinson's disease.
Finally, her powerful presence forced me to discount my pedestrian twitches, irritations and sniffles.
Occasionally, her steps seemed labored,
refusing her call to action.
Still, she visited the colonnaded sites, and waded through rivers of broken stone that illustrated the vulnerability of man's empires.
Throughout her stretch of travel,
she refused rolling chairs, and vetoed helping hands.
And yet, she managed to laugh with spontaneity,
and to join and cheer her fellow travelers on.
Her vigor and enterprise seemed to make the thick,
summer air shimmer. As frothy waves swelled up,
she used the liquid canvas supplied by the Creator
as a writing prompt and scripted a poem celebrating
life and friends.
Eventually, she reserved a day to relax far from the bustle of tourist armies.
Sadly, her fellow travelers felt the immediate shortage of *simpatico*.

If only such valor could be bottled.
I'm still not sure whether it's developed, genetic,
or a combination.
I'm sure that it's truly a tribute to God,
and the unique character He shaped.
It felt so refreshing to splash in the dynamic aura of a life that
refused to open its doors to pessimism and
interruption, always promoting laughter and hope.

Goose River Anthology, 2008

Stop the Train

Coquettish, star dusted freckles
surrounding frolicking azure eyes.
White clam digger pants ostensibly
painted on her balletic body.
Swaying, determined and single minded train,
yet to discover that trains can't fly,
hustles me...far from her scent and sight.
Conductor barks, "Forest Hills!"
Storybook town, torn from a fairy tale book.
Once a peacock basking in glory.
Now, a mere ghost town of racketed memories.
No longer swelling with love games' thrills.
Proud stadium, echoing only memories of Althea, Rod and Pancho.
Today, a feather duster alone in shadow and history.
My aching, dry soul, restrains impotent tears.
An obsessive recurring thought, the feeling of "been there."
She'd kindled my passions, a quarter century plus soul slice.
This geographical machete grinding on steel rails, briefly separating us.
'64 recalled. Stadium brimming with whispering spectators,
Jack-in-the-box heads popping, turning side to side.
Spring, our first date. Cupid dropped his calling card,
and never recalled it. Let me off! Stop the train!
 I need to locate my breezy mate.

Offerings, 3rd Quarter, 1995

Trawler *Trinacria*

I snatched the model, a bow shaped fishing trawler
from the curio store's cluttered shelf.
I rushed that rainbow tinted replica to the cash register,
like an excited child clutching a rediscovered lost toy.
Last century, my mellow Uncle Placido spent hours
 trying to guide my then tiny fingers
to carve these colorful vessels and insert them into bottles.
That man, with hands textured like alligator hide didn't realize that,
in these matters, his nephew qualified as a certified dolt.
Raised in a fishing family that spanned continents and generations,
I often felt like a vegetarian living among carnivores.
I never quite fit, perhaps purchasing this toy boat of my childhood
in this emerging century would now anchor me.
My family's fishing boat served as our second home,
save that ancient superstitions from *Trinacria's Isle*
forbade *Momma's* presence aboard our family boat.
I recall the craft's chaotic cabin, framed and plastered,
with every sanctioned saint, and, of course, numerous replicas
of the saint of saints, St. Anthony (*Sant' Antonio*).
The hot grimy breath of our trawler's burnt coffee maker tilting
atop the pot bellied stove set off a rustle of bodies among the
shivering, teeth trembling fishermen sprawled on the
chilled, plastic coated bunks, crooked cigars dangling from lower lips.
Rustic stoves cooked up a thick, liquorish looking coffee
and a rather clumpy pasta that surprisingly tasted like today's gourmet fare.
Our boat was tied and woven to six others, a family of work boats
linked, tethered, and webbed by a doily of nylon, ribbon-like twines

to help shelter them from squally seas.
This loose federation of threaded boats rocked as one
whenever the seas hiccoughed, and the sea's spasms never took a time out.
The fishing mates on all these prayer card and statue protected
small fishing boats were roughly hewn. They donned baggy pants, green, rubber boots
that nearly reached the navel, topped with flexible gloves that
camouflaged craggy and crinkled hands. Anomalies.
These men were course and hard, yet somehow smooth and soft.
Tough, yet tender, weathered men who occasionally acted like *desperados,*
who tried to cover up and to pray in secret.
They also stealthily delivered free fish to the doorsteps' of the famished.
Above all, these were bona fide Sicilian men of honor who led hard, honest lives.
You see, no one schmoozed or struck deals with the capricious seas.
These muscle laden men, from eighteen to eighty flaunted nicknames like:
Big Nose, the Ugly One, and the Filthy Boy. Nicknames were always articulated upfront.
No haven for sneaks here, and those tagged with less than complimentary names,
created their own mean monikers for their tormentors.
The plastic, disingenuous wallpaper of political correctness
could not catch a breath in this frank and fresh ocean air.

Grandchildren

Happy Trails

Two palm-sized shoes overturned and bellied up,
nestled under the couch,
a yellow embroidered daisy spread across my desk,
a lonesome, drained baby bottle
lying on its side in the dishwasher,
a coloring book filled with defiant creativity,
refusing to accept cuffing by lines,
a chunk of weathered pastel, rolling around the patio,
a bubble wand, floating in the pool without its mated,
soapy bottle, a sleepy sandbox, no longer topless,
pleasantly sealed in my mind's mirror now.
My spouse Adele observes,
"You're gonna find their stuff all over."
She cites her grandmother's heartfelt and clichéd observation.
"Grandchildren provide two joys...
when they come, and, when they go."
I patiently wait to be overwhelmed by the latter.

Candlelight Poetry Journal, Winter, 1997

Shuddering Slave Market Tour

A telepathic alarm linked us.
She locked onto me like a determined laser.
Her dime-sized Sicilian olive eyes
wrapped around my more weathered,
pea sized, black olive eyes.
She then aimed her chin skyward,
and reigned aloof, independent, and proud.
Just moments ago, she'd walked the tourist tour all alone,
yet in the midst of a camera toting crowd.
This receptive eight year-old, driven by the sensitivities of the artist
sown in her soul, hunted me, and strapped her spidery arms
around my waist, every bit as taught as an old salt's knot.
Somehow, the docent's description of the antediluvian slave market
seized a reality and tainted history replayed before our terrified minds,
dripping with the silhouettes of family anguish and agony.
The atrocious ax of outrage wielded by historically brutal scoundrels
separated families forever and severed roots bonded by love.
The screams and yelps of helplessness echoed across the centuries
on a private line to us, and stampeded our souls.
My granddaughter's soft, unwrinkled hand guided me out of the creepy courtyard.
We exchanged looks and both granddad and grandchild failed to repress sniffles.
The two of us, separated by generations, remained bound by bloodline,
simpatico, and island eyes.

Red Hills Reader. Spring, 2004

Turnpike Traffic on My Tile Floor

I tripped on a sandal bridge and twisted my toe
on a turned over tractor trailer jacked up on kiddy flip flops.
That was my 3:00 A.M. collision with toy car land mines, planted
by tiny tots.
Walking in a stupor, I led the growl in my stomach toward the
faithful fridge,
only to feel the throb in my tired and freshly twisted toe and
ankles.
After my shovel-like feet nearly crushed replicas of a '57 Chevy
and the Austin-Healy sports car from my crew cut days,
a few smarting skips, curses, clutches of the foot,
forced me to plop on the kitchen chair to survey the accident
scene.
Aaah, I've ruined a beautiful traffic plan and scattered
three score vehicles toward every corner of that busy floor.
Disrupted traffic patterns popped up all around, designs once
shaped as clearly as Nazca lines by imaginative young minds.
I peek in and see that these kindergarten traffic architects
helped create a modified demolition derby
on those formerly sterile tile floors.
Anger, triggered by torn toes, withers.
A smile slouches across my face.
I desperately want to awaken my grandsons,
shake them out of their dreamland sprawl,
drop to my creaky knees and play cars with them.
Oh well, time for snowy bearded Grump to collect
those toe crunching cars and to rearrange the tile traffic
the same way the grandsons positioned it.

Northern Stars Magazine, March/April 2011

Life's Stretch

Just another crimson faced, shrieking baby.
That act plays and broadcasts everywhere:
in parks, playgrounds, and malls. Nothing unique.
I played the same role a half century ago.
Then, your daughter brings you this new crier, cute fiery, roving eyed
boasting and blasting glass-shattering screams.
Baby stalks, then captures your attentions.
Alone.
Defiantly kicking off boot covers like a soccer star.
She stretches, can't sleep with blankets,
neither can you.
She raises her right woolly brow in a facial question mark,
just like you.
Who taught her that?
It's not an ego thing,
but how did she borrow those gestures?
She's pretty. You're ugly.
She's youthful. You're aging.
She's energetic. You're tired.
Still, you spot traces of yourself
flourishing in this baby.
The cycle continues as the stretch of your life unwraps before you in her brow.

Sicilia Parra, Spring 1996

Grumpa, Gabriella's Dependable Dock

She glides into the balloon stuffed room,
mesmerizes those along her route, and ices time.
She senses the score of eyes, ten gawkers, behind furtive,
peek-a-boo glances.
The eyes somehow strung to her as she traces her steps across
their lives.
Gabriella flashes pirouetting eyes and directs her obedient
Grumpa.
"Hold me now!" she orders.
Wide smiled and honored, her paternal snowy haired fan leaps in
compliance.
"Okay. Enough!" she squeals a few breaths later. "Let me down
Grumpa!"
She then scoots off from corner to cranny, from person to person,
party guest to party guest, in a room incapable of stifling her
spirit and movement.
Gabriella butters and sweetens the overmatched room
with a magic superior to the most skilled politicians. Her eyes
rope her Grumpa,
to make sure that her dock remains loyal and anchored in place.
Moments later, Gabriella tip toes, Bolshoi style, and drifts toward
her granddad.
Once again, she demands, "Hold me!"
The well- seasoned and charmed Grumpa stands,
much like a limp department store mannequin while
Gabriella jumps and wraps around him like an octopus clasping
its prey.
Her hugs and squeezes neutralize his defenses, even if he chooses
to mobilize them.
Gabriella then bolts again like a frenetic filly, holding the
seasoned relative at bay
with a gooey and drippy cheek smooch knotted to dulcet Venus

flytrap stares.
A cliché comes to mind, "Home is where they have to take you in."
Resigned, Grumpa revels in serving as Gabriella's dependable dock.

Alee Oop

Glib, a reputed answer man of sorts.
He's emotionally barren now. Dry.
Hiding behind a shadowy forest of defenses,
his mind suddenly vacuumed of answers too.
Toddler Alee summoned back to steamy Sewanee.
No visions and no magic to massage his pain.
Her smile, now his engaging jailer,
delivered unexpectedly and stealthily into his life.
She tattooed her ambrosial message onto his frosted heart,
and deserted him. She then Alee Ooped his emotions
leaving her gift, his shirt baptized by her cascading tears
to splash his soul, but useless in treating the emptiness in his gut.

Thirteen Poetry Journal, January 1994

Mari

She's a buzz, a swirl, a flood, a flurry of poetic motion.
She's a twirling, perky delight to the eyes, senses and intellect.
She's a blend of soft, of hard,
of decisive and distrustful,
of tender and tough.
She's a high stepping whirlwind.
She engages. She lets go.
She draws crowds, she deflects and dismisses them,
a paradox of confidence and coyness.
When she saunters, a scent of hope
and a dash of confection hitch a ride in her breeze.
One is always in wonder, in awe,
in anticipation of her aura.
Will she smile and ramble my way, or, will she drop step off
in another direction to please other clusters of admirers?
Mari's mom asks, "Why are you kissing my dad's cheek?"
Dancing to her inner conductor she hums,
"Because Grumpa's been a good boy!"
She glides away and Grumpa vows to be good more frequently.

Pyramid International Journal, Fall/Winter, 2010

Golden Gate Miracle

When they tell you it's no big deal, raise your brows.
When they tell you one grandchild covers all, clench your teeth.
When they tell you each new grandchild is same old, same old,
walk away whistling Dixie.
When my tardy, surprise guest Kate made her Golden Gate debut,
a personal *Mardi Gras* resounded in my mind, even for the sixth in cue.
When my informants told me that vengeful gods denied my
having more grandchildren,
when they told me not to expect new links in my family bracelet,
When they told me that my God rarely gave second chances,
I whispered, "You're wrong."
Despite my selfishness,
despite my frivolous words, my prayers materialized.
I told them about my latest miracle,
I told them about my newest grandchild Kate's debut,
the only female tagged with my family name,
a jaw dropping beauty and perfect fit amongst her older cousins.
I told them that her perceptive and magnetically captivating
melting brown eyes and long lashes resided in my family for
generations.
I told them that these traits adorned most other links
in our familial chain.
I told them that after Kate's three squeezes of my wrinkled fingers
and crackling knuckles, she'd seized my spirit and hijacked my heart.

Riversedge Literary Journal, University of Texas, Pan American, Fall, 2011

Nonie's Hand

Petey had known the touch of that hand his entire life,
perhaps in other lifetimes too.
Its delicate touch always comforting, always generous,
always condition free.
From his debut year, while mom and dad worked,
he could always rely on that tender, yet firm hand to shield,
protect, and seamlessly massage his soul.
He squeezed it from his infant seat whenever an alien sound
or terror invaded his space.
He squeezed it when the unfamiliar belching of bellowing trucks,
raging thunder, and the startling new world of screaming sounds
first revealed themselves to the newborn.
Of course, as the years unwrapped, the maturing boy
dismissed his secure clutch, took independent steps into mastering
the wilderness of his new world.
He only remembered Nonie's home base feel
when his soul required strength and an emotional umbilical.
Each day of his life, he wore Nonie's invisible security bracelet of touch.
He could not outrun his genetics, her seeds secured to his body and soul.
Number one in all of her classes, Nonie sacrificed scholarships
and a bevy of other opportunities for her loved ones to succeed.
Her intellectual gifts were freely distributed to her bloodline.
His inherited Killarney eyes, and her trademark freckles painted
his face too.
Nonie's curiosity and stubborn strength cornerstoned his soul.
Her imprint remained a part of the boy.
As a young adult, he vicariously felt its comfort
thru an assembly line of sports wounds,
all problems solved and secured

when Nonie visited the recuperating boy/man and squeezed his hand.
Later in life, he realized that those unrelenting clicks of the clock rudely cratered her face, flurried her hair with avalanches of snowy locks,
while related intruders calloused her once tender touch.
Still, she remained beautiful to the boy.
These were the same hands that cradled poetic chapbooks that bridged centuries.
These were the same hands that taught him the appropriate use of a screwdriver and hammer. These were the same hands that tweaked his
baseball batting skills, and, most importantly,
these were the same hands that helped him survive and respond to the anxieties of a newborn introduced to a mysterious world.
Now, 100 pounds heavier and a foot taller than his slumping grandmother,
with claw-like hands of his own, draped around Nonie's slight hand,
he sensed some vigor abandoning her grip,
a grimace accompanied each tap of her hand now.
Now, it was his turn to cloak,
protect and shroud Nonie and her shrinking hand.

Free Verse, Summer, 2007

Time for Brock Ball

The hirsute schnauzer Sigmund, plastered with Transylvanian brows, knows better.
Brock bobs his head and Sigmund immediately scampers under the closest sofa.
The canine's eyes move side to side, stressed much like those of a ventriloquist's puppet.
Sigmund scrambles, exhibiting the energy of a New York straphanger,
chasing a subway train.
In Bop's den, when the infant Brock, propped up by stanchions of tree trunk like legs,
prances all around that arena, armed with several types of different types of balls,
Sigmund evacuates again.
The scrambling dog claws his way toward the craggy corner or the nearest closet.
Brock's wide eyed, snow bearded Bop, unlike the discerning doggie fails to detect danger.
Perhaps the cavalcade of years used up Bop's entire allotment of quick thinking vouchers.
The surprised Bop finally relocates,
prodded by an avalanche of bouncing balls rebounding off his resilient head.
Granddads don't adapt like dogs.
Sigmund's under couch and closet deployments prove living testimony
as to why the schnauzer breed survived centuries of rodents, plagues,
and other devastating upheavals.
Somehow Brock's tennis racquet swing missed all balls,
and smashed into the boy's own dimpled cheek inscribing a pattern of crisscrossing,

web type lines across his cherubic face.
Despite the racquet's temporary tattoo, a determined smile widens and stretches as Brock looks up red faced.
Nature shortchanged the boy, deprived him of the whining gene. Brock pursues his tactic of clenched teeth and pursed lips to complete his mission.
A new game face imprinted beneath his curly towhead as Brock bounds into Bop's office, tennis racquet chocked in hand. Ignoring pronouncements of society's know-it-all pediatrician about hopping skills developing only after a child's second year, Brock hops across the house.
To slap on finishing touches, he follows that up with a trot and a gallop.
Boy man Brock flings the racquet into a crowded corner.
It bounces, tumbles , and rattles before coming to rest.
Sigmund now runs in circles, looking like a one dog "Ring Around the Rosy" game.
Brock drags an oversized baseball bat in his free hand, resembling a turkey farmer towing an expired, oversized turkey by its neck.
"Bop," he commands, "Ball!"
He directs his granddad with his thick and chunky index finger. The earth has yet to circle the sun twice since Brock's birth, yet, he has the wallop to kick over the old pretzel jar crowded with a diversity of game balls.
They roll lazily over the rug, now littered with a potpourri of spinning spheres.
Brock hands over his racket to a weary Bop, then embraces his ebony baseball bat,
and boldly swings it, further scattering the chaotic crowd of golf balls
covering the pocked rug. Brock's game has yet to be invented. I surmise that it must be a mix of tennis, soccer, baseball, basketball,
and American football. Bop senses that as his seasoned skin

begins to make more Martian canal designs,
euphemistically tagged as character winkles, and, as his body
adopts a more brittle and snowy
Hemingwayesque look, he's convinced that he'll spend many a
day watching Brock pound
a collage of balls in front of adoring crowds of fans, and, of
course, continue engaging and amusing
his wispy haired Bop.

Benji's Brigade

I joined Benji's brigade late.
It seems that all those relatives with rectangular
cosmic ray receptacles resting on lazy laps saw him first.
When that cherubic, moon shaped, ruddy face,
flaunting the welcoming peek-a-boo smile
finally flickered onto my living room screen,
he jangled my mind and I signed onto his brigade of devotees.
Despite all the tangled alleyways life forced me to follow,
the memory of my first moments with my eldest son, Pete,
Benji's dad, resonated in my mind.
Now, a sort of déjà vu crept into my heart.
I recognized that same infectious giggle,
similar raised curious and questioning brows,
the revolving head turn when Pete's Big Sister spoke,
now duplicated by Benji when his Big Sis stirred.
I prayed that the captivating chuckle would always linger with Benji
and that his awe of Big Sis would cuddle him like a lifelong link.
Pete's debut made my day during the Apollo era, as did today's
near repeat performance by Benji on the last days of Space
Shuttle's sallies.
This time, my role revolutionized, from dad to granddad.
What a difference!
This newborn *bambino* just stepped up to life's home plate,
flaunting an identical smile to baseball's famed *Bambino*.
That transformed me into a human jack-in-the box.
I popped up with his every groan, moan, and chuckle on the palm
sized screen.
I'd encountered a mirror-image of that face, during his dad's
debut days
when men pranced across the craggy moonscape taking
glorious steps for all mankind.

The same wide smile, the same chunky hands that grasped,
reached up, groped for the tasty, opened and closed repeatedly.
That's what I saw during my own springtime days,
days when my fingers could still reach a basketball hoop's rim.
Today's communication wonders delivered that familiar
round and radiant baby on a video cupped in my own, creased hands.
It delivered images of my latest grandson to me just a fortnight after his birth.
This newborn entertained me as I reclined in my lounge chair,
thanks to marvels delivered by this latest technology.
Benji flaunted a "How about me folks presence?"
His concerto of cries and symphony of sounds
converted into silly laughter, and eased into my September days.
Despite Benji's distant home, propped beside walls molded into muscular,
broad shouldered Rockies, these mountains barely leapfrogged by gasping airliners
and miles of lace- like highway pavement etched into the Great Plains, were powerless
barriers and could not pry apart this granddad from his youngest grandson.
Mileage itself failed to blockade the boy from his seasoned Bop.
Biblically Benjamin means son of old age, so why not a gift from God
as Bop entered the gray tufted corridors of his days?
Perhaps this baby represents the final link in the Bop's family necklace.
I wish for some sort of eye wipers to clear droplets of happiness
veiling my vision. None of this spontaneous outpouring of one's gut masks
the bond I feel when Benji directs me on my hand-held television.
Welcome home Benji boy!
Just a decade past, I'd not have met, nor loved you so soon.
I'd never have reveled in your chortling concerto,

embraced by hearty laughter.
The shadows of the Rockies, would have separated us .
Praise to this flashing picture pack,
smaller than a cigar carton.
This tiny box broadcasts your broad smile and
instantly delivers your happiness to my Atlantic corner
of the country.
Finally, on one matchless, dazzling day, I wandered into your world
and we met in person.
Previous sleight of hand transformed to authentic magic.
You charmed. You amused me.
You sealed me up, and reeled me in as one of your first fans.
Come now, join your sis and all of your scintillating cousins
and continue carrying the family ball.

Seniors

Marshall Sarah

I slumped in the sun swamped senior center,
waiting for Nanny. Louver doors swung wide,
flapping like bar entrances in Western flicks.
Disorganized, a defeated army of wheelchair
warriors spun in. Arms dangling, heads drooping,
the invasion came to a halt.
Volunteer musicians, playing like volunteers blasted a nostalgic revile.
Life stirred, knarled fingers clicked and danced.
Chairs twirled intermittently, turned 360's.
Vitality and imprisoned rhythms trapped in braided bodies awakened.
Then, she rolled in. Alone.
Head bobbing with commands, the home's Marshall,
a Namibian nightingale.
A star shaped badge proclaiming, "Sarah" was pinned to her shoulder.
Life fermented in this high cheek boned child of Cleopatra.
She celebrated and danced among some of the defeated.
I strolled over and she clutched me with two leathery hands.
Pop bottled lenses failed to camouflage her animated eyes.
She recognized something in her admiring, younger visitor.
"Tell me, how ya been?"
Failing to zip my out-of-control smile, I whispered, "Just fine."
My mind strayed widely wandering about the odyssey of her life.
Born with Marconi's wireless, she romped with the Rough Riders,
watched the kindling and dousing of two tragic World Wars,
outlasted the Union of Soviets, and marched countless times
to prod her homeland toward fairness.
History bowed before her.
The chirpy nurse said, "We're proud of Sarah.
She's our oldest, 105."

"God bless," I whispered, hoping my Nanny,
much like a freshman entering high school,
would pal with the trendy Sarah.
After all, she was popular, admired and a good influence.
Sarah's eyes clamped onto mine and she chanted,
"Praise the Lord!"
Her smile still engaging, she winked, and twirled away briskly.
A stampede followed her.

Riverrun Journal, 1999
Portals, Spring, 2003

Floppy Hair in Sunset Years

The floppy haired one looked familiar, triggering memories as I drove.
That undulating, tufted hair had filled the teen me with jealousy.
I referred to the man as Mr. Mop, since my hair failed the bounce test.
Yes, I'd preferred that bouncy fluff to that wool matting planted on my head.
Mr. Mop regularly crossed my path on my drive from college during my adolescent acne days. A smile now glides across my face at this spontaneous reunion moment.
Today's miscalculated turn reintroduced me to Mr. Mop. Still flopping?
Interrupted flopping now, like a half empty cornfield in a windstorm.
No longer hirsute, shorn by frivolous pages of the calendar.
Mop's remaining hair, clings in desperation,
whitewashed now like the white picket fence embracing his yard.
Reaching for my trusty, steel wool hair, still dripping in ebony,
past jealousies desert me. It all seems so meaningless now,
as if it never existed. Millennium mop leaned on his shillelagh struggling to unwrinkle his body and stand parochial school straight.
Still stooped, he raised his left hand, in a sort of informal salute to the unblemished sky, while choking the garden hose
 in that same hand. That snaky conduit aimed moonward, swamping every in-range plant with his flood event.
I don't remember these plants getting much attention during his fleecier days.
To his right stood a rust colored, clattering basketball hoop, wild grass crept over its cement toes,
while interloping swarms of ants commandeered free housing in the penthouse corners of the basketball rim.

Industrial orange blanketed the tired metal parts.
Last time I passed here, news of Berlin's odious wall crumble
saturated the air waves.
I reminisced about the springtime version of the Mr. Mop
on that historic day.
The same mop, same man, dribbling his ball under the basket
as pre teenagers failed to hinder his bullying path toward the
hoop.
No sprinkling hoses then, no plants to be showered.
No, not hoses, instead tykes of 10 to 12 years,
bouncing basketballs, tugging at his arms and shirt.
The ghosts of an upbeat children's squads chained his arms,
yanked and stretched his jersey as he attempted to launch the
lined ball.
That stereo laughter rumbled and infiltrated my
seemingly sound proof seasoned and sealed Studebaker.
The garden looked after itself, self sufficient then.
Strange how the pushy hands of time,
replete with its unending volley of practical jokes and trickery
repaints the human canvas and reshapes all remaining to be
plowed in her
determined path. The barren garden of decades past now
flourishes like an oasis.
Mr. Mop's cement court is pinned under ringlets of invading
weeds,
while the leader stands devoid of followers, hair,
and his past trappings of leadership.
The orange peel backboard sheds more than a seasoned dog in
July, and children are presently so alien to the yard that radar
needs deployment to discover the closest child.
All that remains of that scene are a few strands of silky hair,
a wrinkled, gaunt basketball,
and a stooped man with a pained smile and a full heart.

Perigree Literary Journal, January, 2005

Fantasy Camp

Legendary sport names carved atop the craggy stadium
survived countless Great Lake snows.
Names riveted to, and etched in grainy, freckled stands peer down
from the top deck perch of the weary, Motor City ball field.
Silent rafters witnessed the agility of Cobb, Kaline, Kell, and Greenberg.
A grin plastered my face as I recalled my lucky Ruthian clout
that ricocheted off the 370 foot marker.
No doubt, the wings of my protective angel deposited my hit there.
How else?
Those same invisible divinities declined to tame my huffing,
 nor lubricate my creaky legs while I lumbered 'round the bases
at tortoise speed.
Camp closing, at least, I'd gasped baseball's signature smells
of leather gloves, turf, freshly sliced grass, and hot dogs.
The fuzzy faced rookie journalist, positioned to my left
resembled a reincarnated Satchel Paige, until his baseball toss exposed
his ruse. Not a trace of darts, or dances in his hurls.
I heard that same scribe sing his solo,"Rizzuto, Gates, Mickey,
they all played right here."
I peeked over at that tuneless tenor, his jarring, unmusical litany
faded into the cool, silent breeze.
I reeled my curious eyes back to their sandy sockets,
and protected my hot corner.
That first hit targeted me.
It seemed shot from a cannon as it skidded over coifed, mahogany dirt.
Fortunately, it swerved suddenly.
I dived like an Olympic swim racer.

I glared into the pit of my leather mitten and,
my mouth stretched wider when I saw the captured baseball.
A snow cone look-alike settled in my glove.
"Major league, just like Aurelio," screeched Manager Gates.
Three score men stooped, most sporting maternity sized shirts,
billboarding name and number of their favorite,
faded legendary superstar on their liniment lathered backs.
Most these mirror headed, milky bearded dugout raconteurs,
lugged a duffel bag full of dreams and cheered at the shadow
of themselves in each fellow camper.
Showers dry.
Nightfall draped the field.
Still connected to cleats, I crackled onto the dusty baseball
diamond one last time.
I squinted toward left field...
7:10 P.M., on the dream ballpark scoreboard.
Dream materialized. Dream ended.

Angel News, April/May/June 1999
Baseball Bard, 2013

View from the Balcony

I don't know exactly when I started my climb
toward life's balcony seats.
Were I at a baseball game, I'd qualify as a bleacher bum,
camping in the eye straining, cheap seats.
I can barely pinpoint when I was shuffled to
the irrelevant neighborhood of life.
Retirement? Suppose I should be grateful
since many of my teammates never even scraped their toes
on this spiral staircase of the distant stands.
These bleacher seats of life, reached only by a one-way
stairwell molded from the craggy mortar of accumulated years.
Save that, I thought that I'd always be center stage,
initiating action, a life player.
Perhaps, I'd already emptied myself on that playhouse below
while *la dolce vita* simmers and remains.
Nowadays, from my distant perch I watch replacement players.
Some are even recognizable.
Have I become a cheerleader, a voyeur of life,
living and rooting for those haughty hedonists
occupying the stage, while I, in effect, have become a pom pom waver
of sorts contributing merely concerted cheers?
Do they know that I've been baptized by the sweat of sacrificial ancestors?
The players all move, all participate, all smile, even occasionally look up
and waive at me-patronizingly.
I suppose it's a counterfeit deference to my seemingly snowy
Hemingway-style mane.
I suppose this is good.
I suppose I've lumbered toward my chill out phase.
Or, am I squatting in the foyer of my frozen out stage?

At least my view of past, present, and future life is clearer
than when I thoughtlessly pranced across the midlife stage below.

Free Verse, #86, 2006

School

School's Out

I stare out of my lifeless classroom,
students vacuumed out by summer's calendar.
Flaking bulletin boards surround me. I gape thru my veined window,
no piles of tepee shaped snows confront me today.
Instead the tarred, ribboned, school road stop steams like a volcano.
Its zephyr gently massages the school's extremities.
A half dozen slumbering busses, painted like Easter eggs,
flaunt ebony braided sides. These shaky busses slink in silently,
awaiting the liberation of the teen celebrants.
These powered, portable egg cartons stand ready to seal,
ready to stamp, ready to file away still another school year.
Pungent goldenrod wafts thru my cubicle
while a crazed, headache inducing machete machine,
harnessing a wiry fish line spins wildly, mutilating fauna.
Déjà vu. That sharp odor of liberated golden weed
blankets the thick June air reminding me of Ebbets Field summers,
days of capricious changing voices, acne faced ball field warriors
playing on junkyard city lots, posing as baseball fields.
My thoughts raced to shiny, ebony hardballs enveloped
in electrical tape, drawn tighter than a tourniquet.
I could feel those splintered bats of old held in place by screws,
and imagined seedy playing fields carved by kids, for kids.
The screaming machines lifeline is yanked, ending the wild weed slasher's
rasping opus. Now, it's time for school bell squeals and teen yelps.
Verity buffets me again, "SCHOOL IS OUT!"

Zillah Poetry, Winter, 2002

Sat Shuffle

Stereo sniffles and backward capped teens.
Students sitting guru style. Assorted thinker-like poses.
Fists supporting sagging chins.
Pages shuffle. Frustration!
Erasures scrub and bleach pages.
Feet tap to discordant private symphonies.
Gurgling stomachs complain.
Sweat drains. Frantic backs of hands rub noses roughly.
Temporary blemished faces seem stitched with worry lines.
Second hour sniffles spread.
Coughs change, more baritones, more like drum rolls.
An excuse me, novice cough joins the chorus.
Its stammering and staccato sounds like a faltering engine.
Aerobics time. A neck exerciser performs a solo audition.
Two long, fat-free arms strangle his neck like a vise.
He jerks violently, chiropractor style.
The exam's math section induces a calculator concerto.
A gum gnasher chomps his solo,
The class choir recited, "God bless" at the sneezer's cue.
Arms up like an umpire's tornado like signal for home run,
She pleads, "Tissues please!"
Mr. Proctor wonders whatever happened to the joy of learning?
Fun is unwelcome an uninvited guest in this Test Center.
"Time is up!"proctor shouts with painted smile.
He smiles, "Last time baby!"

Northern Stars Magazine, June 2000

Daisy in the Poet's Den

I sat silently.
Guarding your poetic yelps.
A teacher just stripped of students,
my score of successful years as a blackboard brigadier
disregarded.
The school wardens severed me.
Fired for financial factors.
I fled to the writer's workshop and dreamed of
rekindling slumbering, or scraping for secret talents,
desperately drilling for rediscovery.
But you Daisy, you attended for different reasons.
You represented an unseasoned celebration of sonnets.
Your gossamer incantations promoted zephyrs of hope.
You waltzed into the workshop,
eyes ablaze at meeting your giants of American letters
face-to-face.
They were your heroes at 17, just as DiMaggio and Robinson were
to the 17 year-old child in me.
You expected that workshop poets would gently caress your
metrical hand
and lead you to the wonderland of poetry's big leagues.
You sketched spirited, sunny sonnets.
You inhaled images of shimmering streams, flowered ponds,
and God's wonder.
Jaded adult lecturers championed death and desolation.
I agonized over the smug tar brushing of your unsheltered muse,
by your jaded heroes, the usual brash academic bullies.
Rudely released by academia myself, why should I care?
I sat and witnessed the battering of your delicate word paintings,
by the supposed sages of my generation.
In reality, Vietnam's living victims, weaned on memories
of that leech infested battleground.

Somehow, these survivors of those dreary days
became pedantic persecutors and muggers of upbeat poetry,
opponents of optimism.
And yet, they sit before us sheltered by a flimsy umbrella of fame,
while you search their words seeking nonexistent insights and
false gods.
Since my release from duties as a school's hired hand,
once selected to nurture and teach springtime talent,
why should I care if my contemporaries sully your poetic soul?
So what if the hardened, free love misogamists that Vietnam spat
out
shatter your spirited verses.
At the workshop's closing, I asked, "How was it, Daisy?"
Like a battered spouse in denial, she said, "Great!"
Astounded, I briskly walked away muttering about the resilience
of youth
and groaned, "Why should I care?"

Northern Star Journal, March/April 2000

Cell Phone Regatta

All of those hours, in all those geometry classes of my fuzzy-faced days,
never prepared me for such a landlocked regatta of triangles.
A quarter century of participation in school openings failed to expose me
to such a diverse array of staccato marchers packed with animated walkers.
A half century of gym workouts never presented me with such a soufflé of biceps: Balloon shaped...Striated ...Flabby...
Today's opening day of college leaves me surrounded and scrambling
as I bring up the rear of a brigade of lumbering, yet,
paradoxically energetic coeds, all unconcerned,
all mellow despite impending tardiness.
All flaunt triangulated arms.
Of course, each triangle is unique, but each directs the index finger to plug into the ear.
Coeds laugh, giggle, pause, walk with missteps, and engage in debates with phantom opponents.
Face-to-face debate is nowhere to be found, not in this cell phone century.
They use free hands to point, to inscribe an imaginary loop in the thick August air.
This parade reminds me of the "make a muscle" poses of my school yard days.
I look around toward my future collegians.
In a few seconds, I'd poke a hole in the cellular walls enveloping me and demand
disconnect and quiet, even risky verbal swordplay to stake claim to my lesson
by debilitating the focal point of communication triangles.

Free Verse, 2007

Angelica's Articulations

"Professor," Angelica exhaled from behind hesitant and clenched teeth.
"Is this the correct word that is required?" She stammered slightly.
This inquisitive immigrant strained her words between her tongue and cheek,
desperately hoping to shake out the best and most appropriate choices.
Finally, they dripped softly from her lavish lips.
Initially, her word sifting seemed as exhausting and labored
as a clam digger shaking out undersized clams thru a discriminatory screen,
save that Angelica's arena remained reserved for the arts.
She was obsessed with expressing the best, most exact words to her mentor.
Only these select words drained from her verbal strainer.
Her flushed cheeks partnered with an embarrassed plea, "Excuse me, I don't speak so well this English."
The professor fixed his eyes and triangulated, elevated brows on her.
Angelica reluctantly released an esoteric, five syllable English word, and dared to plead for forgiveness after these verbal jewels slid off her tongue, fearing traces of mispronunciation.
The professor winked and said, "Your word choices honor my profession.
They prove that I'm the beneficiary of a uniquely rewarding job, because a well-tuned line, a fresh line, energizes and clarifies the language.
We're all better off for that."
Angelica wrinkled her forehead and peek-a-booed her face behind long and lean piano player fingers.
She danced out of the room sporting a beet tinted complexion

and a hangdog mouth that
was happy, but speechless.

Attitudes/Encounters

Lost in the World

If only he'd not unwrapped her swaggering personality
from his crush of college coeds.
Now, she flittered away like a shadowy radar image
from a raging jet plane, and, even on this shrinking planet,
she'd gone missing.
For a tad the magic of electronics served as a communication
life raft. Eventually, she yanked anchor
and short circuited transmissions.
He felt strangely relieved,
strangely relieved of worry,strangely relieved of responsibility,
strangely relieved, that the stress of her success no longer piled
on his back. A bullying nimbus cloud of disappointment tried to crowd
his space so, instead of enjoying his emancipation,
her escape from his world flushed his gut,
much like a Shakespearian protagonist,
darting phantasms scrambled in his head.
He wondered: Does she walk here?
Will she appear here?
Cruel and empty illusions teased as they rallied in his reverie.
Once again, he felt tormented.
If only they'd not locked eyes and exchanged ideas.
That, however, would have aborted or blockaded
the dozens of odes her physical scent
scattered about his inspirations and writings.

Northern Stars, November/December, 2011

Soothing Human Alarm Clock

My human alarm clock silenced,
curling pillows of salty waves smother her muffled voice,
lost somewhere in the land of the fjords.
Every sunrise, from across the *alto mare*,
I was the benefactor of her wake up verse
transmitted by invisible 21 st Century drumbeats.
This daily and reliable celestial messenger inlaid my day with gusto.
Last night, she seemed to surface in my slumber,
softly flitting thru a field of sunflowers.
How disappointing to awaken to illusion and nothingness
as bleak as the holes in misplaced galaxies.
Long ago, she lured me with her look.
Soon after, she reeled me in with magical metaphors.
And now, a grating silence scrapes my soul.
I miss her daily brain teaser.
I miss her passion for unwrapping the new day.
I miss her saccharine wake-up message.
I sit sandwiched between cacophonies of unrelated lawn mowers
screaming at the sultry air surrounding them
and try to savor her easy verse.
I sit staring at my hibernating pool,
not ready to shed its canvas ebony overcoat
while pangs of poetic deficits cause me to yearn
for my Nordic nomad.
Her lyrics spoke of our belonging
to the same community of dreamers,
and I felt willingly trapped within her *dolceria* of verbs,
adjectives and shuffling thoughts.
She's retreated back to her nest and because of that,
I'm sure that European lovebirds chirp more boldly,
and its swans sport plumage to celebrate their vagabond's return.

As for me, the concerto diffuses and her aria circles
and recircles my mind.
This maestro smirks as he searches aimlessly
for his unique *LaScala* of metaphors.

DC Tearoom

The stringy haired woman slinks into her October teahouse seat.
Lazy eyeglasses reclining on a carved nose bridge,
book spread on her inviting lap,
like a drying tee-shirt on a clothesline.
She sips and sloshes herb tea, folds her tongue
as it slowly brushes her lower lip
so as not to miss one savory taste,
driving me to plunge my nose into my teacup.
The snoopy eyed, shaggy coed claws, slashes, and digs
into her Frisbee shaped purse and glances at this gaping poet
aware of the dual tangles pressing her moment,
her purse and my improbable admiration.

Carefree like her flapped sisters of the Roaring Twenties,
splashed with flower girl vestiges too,
yet harnessed in the 21 st Century.
The beats of the previous centuries 60's high notes
float thru the tattered room curtains
and ooze into her vibrant soul as she collapses into her book
dismissing her intellectual voyeur.
Were I those melodies for just a moment?

Byline Magazine Contest, April 2001, Honorable Mention

The Whistling Door and My King Lear Moment

The storm bully huffed and blew into town for a third installment.
Old hat now, he'd punished these people, animals, and turf
before.
He'd shoved and toppled trees, homes, simultaneously trampling
dreams.
He'd roared and rumbled by in staccato style, wheezing, and
boasting blowhard breaths, leaving a sloppy trail of terror on
saturated, sticky streets.
Countless cowering victims peeked from the shadows of streaked
windows, declining to move an arm's length out their doors
toward driveways
where plastic capped, hooded unread newspapers awaited rescue.
My schnauzer pleaded to go into the driveway of swirling clutter.
Only a foot out the door, with just a sample dosage of buffeting,
he changed his mind, brushing me hard with prickly hair
as he scrambled back and away from doggie outhouse.
Disappointed by his fear, I tugged, and the dog scraped
his stubborn nails into the ground, grinding toward his outdoor,
doggie restroom.
A soaking breeze streaked and slid around conducive corners in a
failed ambush.
Pines, oaks, and palm trees bent more conspicuously than yoga
masters.
Plants swayed and succumbed, submissive like defeated
surrendering soldiers.
Escaping and undisciplined tendrils of water slashed and
indiscriminately whipped.
Yesterday's stately trees shimmied, curtsied, and tipped their
branches too.
Animals groped, dug, and tunneled while cranes wailed after
losing lifetime loves.
Lakes quivered, and accepted heaps of refugee materials evicted

by the wind.
A baby palm tree kneeled, downcast and facing the rumpled golf green.
Exposed, a family's first home, a dream, with its roof yanked, stretched and discarded across the hapless, golfer free course.
This diffident victim emboldened.
As doggie boy sat, terrorized and frozen in place, once again, fists clenched, I burst out the whistling door.
Snooty schnauzer surprisingly followed, now defying the bullying blowhard.
We struggled to confront the faceless, waterlogged monster.
Immediately, cascades of crazed water with pellets of delinquent moisture
and collected chunks of rubbish along with its hijacked booty, pinpricked our legs. We stood bonded, facing fiendish storm.
I cursed, schnauzer turned around, spun his legs wildly.
Taut leash kept him from returning to sanctuary without completing his business.
My eyes blinked, but refused to shut as colonnaded bursts of hail hunted us.
I raged back at the hurricane acting like, a modern-day Lear with a bold sneer, much like an animated pro football official, I flailed my arms and screamed, in what seemed a King Lear moment.
"Come on you wimp! Is that your best? We'll just stand here, and see what you've got tough guy!"
A muffled rumble of thunder gurgled among the distant palms.
Surely, I'd tweaked his rage. Escaping ringlets of water slashed and whipped, an uprooted tree began to roll toward us, like a blowing beach ball in a summer squall.
The offended and enraged hurricane continued to push us around,
while rumbling tree and his swirling support cast focused on me.
I yelped, "Retreat!"

Riversedge Poetry Journal, University Texas, Pan American, Spring 2009

Lobster Duck

The stiff- necked princess sailed sleekly, willowy and proudly
outstretched upon her ice pond throne,
until Lobster Duck chugged her way.
She scrambled off, stutter stepped, ungracefully evicted by
Lobster Duck.
The remaining geese and ducks waddled past pond icebergs
to greet my food filled human hand at pond's shoreline,
impatiently squawking and lining up at my portable bread line.
Doggie peeked from behind my legs,
until a frightened goose sprinted away. My daring dog soon
realized
that geese were supposed to cower in his presence.
And so began our ritual of strolling pond side, and our daily
routine
of visits from geese and ducks, and Doggie's bullying, chasing
snow sprint.
One day, after dispensing proud princess again,
Lobster Duck pranced onto shore.
A head shorter than all the other pond birds, this dumpy faced
duck,
with the look and texture of a lobster swaggered out of the water,
rumbled and strutted along stony path.
She greeted me by holding my eyes in an intimidating magnetic,
visual grip. Her glare, as scary as any handshake I'd ever grasped
from any macho man.
Doggie sensed the moment to assume top breed status.
He pranced over toward Lobster Duck. Time to bully the arrogant
bird.
The Quasimodo of the bird world was impatient with imposters
and,
despite the added weight of a score of grotesque warts
pasted to beak and face, waddled my wimp doggie off,

along with his band of web toed pals.
Lobster Duck bumped up next to me,
rubbed her grainy bill on my knee,
then glared up like a heavyweight boxer at weigh-in time.
She measured me.
Every glacial day, at sunrise, during that arctic New England February,
Doggie raced away while Lobster Duck saluted me with a long stare.
After a surprise, premature thaw melted away some snow,
Lobster Duck disappeared.
A fortnight late, I approached a busy duck feeder.
She reminded me of a spinning water sprinkler scattering bread instead of water.
I asked her, "Have you seen the Lobster Duck?"
"No, haven't. Actually, I'm worried about her," she said.
We looked at each other like old friends who'd lost a chum.

Perigee Literary Journal, January, 2005

Look What I Found

The winsome Adriatic zephyr sliced across the ocean liner,
Neptune's water anchored me several hundred kilometers
from Aristotle's motherland.
Sleep eluded me as I stretched twisting, and tossing on A Deck.
Words scribbled on the ship's itinerary sheet flapped before me,
rattling like baseball cards clipped to bicycle spokes
while this muscular ocean soothed body and soul.
And, so it ended...
The noisy, restless, nocturnal sea along with its stalking,
glittery rooftop stars reminded me of curtain calls to friendships.
It all started few hundred kilometers from here
on a leafy land populated by impractical poets and idealistic dreamers,
stimulated by casual chatter which evolved into delightful banter.
Finally, a soul searching discourse amongst friendly fellow travelers
closed the chapter.
Earlier, the newer friends and familiar old pals experienced the exhaustion
and loneliness of the shaggy and wounded August mutt
hobbling across the Acropolis, all alone.
Why? Why this empty gut feeling? My friends walked and scattered
within arm's reach but thoughts of our shared past and our old
celebrations new discoveries and foolhardiness too strutted into
my day.
Glimpses. Peek-a-boo reminders of minutes of sharing,
adolescent giggles, serious concerns, hope and hopelessness occupied
my thoughts.
Sheltered somewhere between the stubborn rock and sway of this ship,

an eerie sense of loss regarding both old and new friends shrouded the moment.
Sadly, the aura of Athena's temple, just a gull's range away, stood bereft of relief, or solace.

Sand Castle Seiges

It's the law of the summer sands,
an unwritten seacoast commandment.
It's the print less and voiceless decree of Kiddy beach.
Unguarded sand castles must be booted by marauding munchkin feet.
Adult military folk camouflage this operation by calling it sanitizing.
Aware of the unwritten law, I followed and watched
a cadre of five year-old plunderers reconnoiter sunset beach.
Sure enough, these wreckers razed every sand castle in their path,
until they wandered by the queen of castles.
Rangy and stately as an expansive beach blanket,
protected by grainy, carved moat,
a dozen well-shaped parapets raised four levels,
with a slick staircase of shells and walls buttressed with starfish
or mortared with sand and ocean salts.
Its seaweed lawns spread out between trees made up of wandering weeds and reeds.
The castle sat as pompously, as a Kalahari lion lounging on a cliff
while hovering over its domain of barren sands.
The demolition squad abolitionists strutted and walked around its walls
looking like scrutinizing used car buyers about to drop kick tires.
They scooped out some moat sand, and scattered it as they walked away
granting the castle pardon to co-exist until the turnover of tides.

Zillah Poetry Journal, Spring, 2009

Computer Calisthenics

Her fingers felt as soft as an over soaked bar of soap.
Long, slim, as zesty as Ziegfeld legs.
Tapping to a desktop meringue.
Sporting a Michelangelo flair, reminiscent of some of
his most memorable marble masterpieces, she'd
squeezed from the womb barely two decades past.

Her fingers were created to delight a piano with their aerobic
stretch.
Her fingers were created to delight the canvas with their soothing
stroke.
Her fingers were created to delight the beneficiary of their
melodic massage.

She stretched forward, in a 45 degree lean toward her computer,
fingers following and supporting her callisthenic bridge.
The lithe body now appeared as supple as a smooth as an arching
wave.
Tight blue jeans fought their futile fight
to contain the impudent sweater clamoring for freedom.

A stubborn sweater boldly peeped out
and charged up her dotted, ivory back.
Tomato faced, she yanked it down and
fixed on my chubby fingers which masked
my "caught in the act" look,
her eyes blinked and blinked again.

Riversedge Literary Journal (U. Of Texas Pan-American), Fall, 2003

Vagabond Flower

She blossomed in unfamiliar fields.
Fields alien, even to his most pregnant visions.
Her pastures, so different from those of his daybreak days,
yet her bloom dazzled too.
And my, my, the diorama in his head scrambled,
overmatched by the wonder sprouting before it.
Perhaps she was an escapee,
or a loner from a hidden heaven, or Shangri-La.
Watching her limber limbs scoot off to pound the beach
volleyball,
bedazzled him like a foolhardy teenager trying to tame
and contain his first crush.
Certainly adolescent sport was never like this.
Faced with the foolishness of a winter leopard,
captivated by springtime sass, he couldn't help but wonder
if her earthy debut had been scheduled just a few decades sooner,
might he be returning her serve?

Offerings Poetry Journal, Third Quarter, 2004

And Now, the Breeze Shadows Siggy

And, so it ended like this.
Cold, so, so, cold. It wasn't supposed to.
Throughout his life, Siggy looked to me to deflect his terrors:
thunder, lightning, and frothing monster dogs.
I'd rescued him from all his nightmares.
Now, I stand holding his ashes, next to his favorite siesta spot, the
Ninth Hole.
Memories of lugging my first dog Cocoa in and out
of my boyhood bungalow on his sunset day, still haunted me.
Had history repeated? These same arms of mine,
were about to carry my sagging Siggy to his executioner.
That dormant, and dreadful dream returned as Siggy
started to silence.
Recently, I'd carried my schnauzer onto his backyard golf course
on a daily basis.
No sprints lately. No swagger. No whirling dervish. Nary a
prance in his gait.
Legs locked and bowed, he plopped on the green where he'd
chased
the invisible breezes and attacked his personal windmills.
He sits, long faced, wearing a sort of cloistered nun's meditative
stare.
His world, as eerily silent as a monastery.
He rotates his head in slow motion, gazes like a teary widow
scouring the ocean for her missing mariner.
I clap my hands several times before Siggy senses it,
he finally totters toward me in a labored manner,
an aching expression posted across his face,
much like the grimace of a gang tackled football running back.
My dog's bulging eyes peek at me behind an interrupted,
flimsy veil, a symbolic, closing curtain . I tap him softly.
He totters toward a distant knoll as renegade tears fall from my

eyes.
I cradle him and head back home, trying to stall his moment with mortality.
For over a decade a nudge from his prickly nose served as my daily alarm.
Roles now reversed, if I fail to awaken him, he snores thru lunch.
There was a time when he barked repeatedly to get my attention, a time when he flipped his dish on the floor demanding food.
None of that now, a form of doggie Alzheimer's hushed his bark.
I've not heard his woffs or growls for the last three rainy seasons.
Siggy staggers and waddles past my desk, draping his chin over my toes.
Guided by Braille radar, the dog prods me and fancies himself a healer.
Somehow he instinctively tracks a scab sticking to my knee.
Without seeing it, his healing sandpaper tongue disinfects the wound.
As he nurses my leg, I recall the day his brashness, growls, and penash was
squelched after he offended his adopted brother, Ebony the Greyhound.
Siggy soon dangled from the doggie high rise of Ebony's mouth.
His skyscraping, step -sibling taught him respect on that bumpy jaw ride.
I see images of Siggy taking Ebony's pillow in his mouth,
and carrying it for months after the Big Dog's final breath.
I also felt a crush of sadness when he started losing his senses,
and so I braced for his last voyage.
Unlike the days of his huddling in my shadow during a thunderstorm,
his ultimate journey took place without the company of this sidekick.
I shut my eyes and minutes later, a slobbery, grainy dog tongue is unexpectedly back to work brushing my face.
Siggy scrambled and deposited his tattered, toy snake in my lap.

His nose, now dry as an Arabian desert, tacitly ordered me to play.
Somehow, my dog seemed infused with newfound energy.
Sad, no more games awaited him.
I'd enjoyed our games and moments, as much as he had.
Ultimately, despite barricades,
my wandering Siggy went out
flailing and dramatically with the glory of a Cyrano.
He simply bashed down the pool gate,
and leapt into the pool for one last time.
His ultimate sleep awaited and he'd
devised his own plan, on his own terms.
Siggy left us all, maintained his dignity,
devised his own conditions,
silenced forever by the cooling pool.

Riversedge Literary Journal (University Of Texas, Pan-American, Spring, 2010)

Emerald Isle

Sibling Celebration

The home plate sized and gooey, ebony cake announced, "Happy Bicentennial Bill and Dot?"
Gnarled fingers interlocked in a loving hand lock.
Clamped to her nonagenarian baby brother like a human vice, big sister tugged him toward her, repeating a rehearsed scene from Flapper times.
He turned away looking like the ripest Macintosh Apple.
Frowning and curling her brow at his "cool" body language, she yanked his arms in like an obstinate horse's reins.
Was this to be the final squeeze for the surviving, wrinkled grapes on the December vine?
An invisible, silent communication oozed between the twin set of clouded eyes.
Their stares excluded all others from their private recital,
in this, the winter of their collective near two century marathon.
Four generations spilled out of the palm-lined party room surrounding them.
Laughter exploded and off color jokes proliferated.
Children screeched, babies bawled, and parents chastised.
Meaningless football images sauntered across the scratchy screen.
None of that traffic detoured the seasoned soul mates.
Their arms linked, minds united, in a run-on replay of youth.
Big sister framed little brother's face inside her crinkled bony hand,
and softly pressed her lips to his nose.
Oblivious to the cratered curse squatting on their faces, oblivious to runaway teeth,
oblivious to detoured tales trapped within the cavernous earwax, they cuddled, silently reflecting on their shared lives.
Interloping music racketed.
Finally, they unwrapped, defying rusted bodies, and they

stiffly stood.
Heads up and proud they shared their ultimate shuffle, a staccato sputtering Irish Jig, while preparing for a looming reunion in Killarney's patch of Paradise.
The rude and disrespectful banditry of age failed to snatch or even detour their effervescent spirits.

Goose River Anthology, 2011

Sunday Pig Tails and Donuts

She skipped toward the saccharine sacred altar,
shamrocks dotting her dress,
fingers stretched, hanging on her dad's coat,
her bouncy butterscotch tinted pigtail flopping side to side,
bounding, without restraints.
I watched, filled with envy.
Was it so long ago?
My own pig-tailed lassie wearing weathered,
open-mouthed sandals, clung to my patched corduroy
jacket,
on God's Visitor's Day Sundays.
No longer do we share the sweets of Sunday's jellied donuts.
Time bullied its way between us, pried us apart.
Memories of crimson powdered bakery delicacies
sealed tight in white boxes,
pinched by candy stripped strings dangling from
tiny, poked ceilings are all that remain.
I hope that every papa soaks up all of Sunday's sweet
nectar.
I vowed to revisit the old bakery after church
and order two dulcet jellied donuts once again,
missing my sassy pigtailed lassie.

Candlelight Poetry Journal, Spring 1997

Alfresco With Catarina

On a battered bench beneath the austere Aran Isle sky,
she squeezed in next to him and crowded his Irish stage.
He loved it.
Hardly a time and hardly a place to discover a surprise treasure,
he thought.
Her beauty rubber banded well beyond the mere physical.
Blessed with an endless supply of the most striking women
framing his world, the seasoned professor sensed a sophisticated,
a layered beauty in Catarina.
She'd chronicled her lyrical survival story in the land of the story-
tellers.
Somehow, none of the reputed native raconteurs told their tales
better.
Now, three full moons later, disconnected by Atlantean
barriers
of place and time, he missed her taunts and her tease.
He missed her daily, somewhat profound quote.
His illusions began unraveling too.
This Australian artist's hand fashioned gifts for lumbering
tourists, yet
she failed to present the professor with any lasting, gift wrapped
treasures.
He rapidly realized that she was not a channel to his Holy Grail.
Cartarina, peerless in her desolate, slate mountaintop
outpost that continually
dribbled granite into the spitting and snarling sea below,
still failed to approach replicating his eternally
seventeen-year old Adele from an abandoned century.

Riversedge Literary Journal (U Of Texas Pan-American), Spring 2003

Misplaced?

It seemed that everything he'd seen on the isle within
the Emerald Isle was framed and fenced in rock,
in stone, or in slate.
It provided a prohibitive and stifling environment
for his flamboyant Sicilian soul.
Petey's emotions poured out onto life's stage
like a bleeding inkblot.
He wondered how history's best sculpted women,
personally molded by the Goddess Bronwyn,
accepted, as sanctuary,
such an oppressively dank and stony canvas.

Northern Stars, September/October 2009

Shamrock Scamper

Festival ended. All the hoopla and hullabaloo took wing
like feathers caught in the cascade of an autumnal huff.
Now, my role reduced to scrap collector.
I took down and removed three dozen triangulated balloons
and liberated them to air out in the fleecy sky.
Just then, she targeted me and skipped my way with sparkling
eyes and gestures collecting smiles from everyone in her path.
The giant shamrock pinned to her shoulder screened
all but the child's face.
She stared me into submission.
I followed her unspoken command,
and approached the angel incarnate flashing her ivory,
picket fence teeth, choreographing those near her
from behind grape-sized, azure eyes.
"I thought you'd want this bunch of balloons," I whooped.
Her freckles merged, her eyes expanded, nearly bulged.
Gawking, I wondered when they'd outreach human limits.
Rattling the floating pyramid, she lip-synced, "Thank you,"
while hiding behind a peek-a-boo glance.
Definitely, a precious moment to replay for a lifetime.
I thought back to the one of the earliest Pope's first sightings
of these lassies from Limerick.
He was right, if her great-great grannies flaunted Shamrock Girl's
face,
then, these women were indeed a race of cherubs.

Riversedge Literary Journal (U Of Texas Pan-American), Spring 2003

About the Author

F. Anthony D'Alessandro retired after a 34 year teaching career in New York State. For a quarter of the century, he served as a high school newspaper advisor. For several years he was an associate editor of the now defunct *Italo–American Times*. Since his retirement from high school, he has taught at Dowling College, New York Institute of Technology, Valencia College and the University of Central Florida. His combined tenure at Dowling College and the University of Central Florida resulted in his training a platoon of teachers. A former educator of the year, D'Alessandro currently serves as a coordinator for student teachers at the University of Central Florida.

D'Alessandro's writings have appeared in *Chicken Soup for the Father's Soul, Modern Bride, Teaching K-8, American School Board Journal, Newsday, San Francisco Chronicle, Christian Science Monitor, Tampa Tribune, Principal, Mature Living Magazine, Goose River Anthology*, and *Friends' Anthology*. After successfully accomplishing his dream of running with the bulls in Spain, he published his essay "A Coward's Guide to Running with the Bulls" in the Winter, 2000 issue of *Spectacle Literary Journal*.

He married his beautiful Celtic sweetheart Adele 48 years ago. She blessed him with three wonderful children. Oldest son Pete is an NBA executive, his daughter Mary-Kim delights in being a kindergarten teacher, and his youngest son Jon relishes a career as teacher and coach. D'Alessandro thoroughly enjoys his grandchildren and has written poetry about each of them. Their ages range from 2 to 22.

A native of Brooklyn, brought up by Sicilian speaking parents, he remembers his roots. He credits legendary baseball announcers Red Barber, Mel Allen, and Vince Scully for teaching him English. He still follows his sainted mother's advice, "Anthony, always do the right thing."

www.ingramcontent.com/pod-product-compliance
Lightning Source LLC
Chambersburg PA
CBHW030326080526
44584CB00012B/726